LEVEL E

CALCULATOR MATH

Gerardus Vervoort and Dale J. Mason

Fearon Teacher Aids

An imprint of Paramount Supplemental Education

Executive Editor: Carolea Williams

Editor: Christine Hood

Cover and Inside Design: Rose Sheifer

Illustration: Corbin Hillam

ISBN 0-86653-880-1

Printed in the United States of America
1. 9 8 7 6 5 4 3 2 1

Preface

I have always endeavoured according to my strength and the measure of my ability to do away with the difficulty and tediousness of calculations, the irksomeness of which is wont to deter very many from the study of mathematics.

John Napier
From the *Dedication of Rabdologiac*

This comment by the inventor of logarithms still applies today. Manipulation of numbers is not the prime objective of an arithmetic program—in fact, it is only a minor part. People must know *when* to multiply and subtract as well as *how* to multiply and subtract. They also must know what information is required to solve a problem and whether a proposed answer is reasonable.

Problem solving is the essence of mathematics and it is here that we find the calculator's value to the mathematics program. With calculators eliminating the drudgery of lengthy calculations, students can concentrate on the problem-solving process. Here are some specific situations where calculators are useful.

- Estimating, or mentally grasping the overall proportions of an operation, is an essential skill. Calculators enable students to make estimates and then rapidly get feedback on their answers. Interestingly, while calculators facilitate the development of estimating skills, they also increase the need for that ability, for minor operating slips or low batteries can easily produce incorrect answers. Users must therefore develop a feeling for what the answer to a problem should be and critically examine the answers displayed. *Calculator Math Levels A-E* contain a series of activities to improve the student's ability to find approximate answers to addition, subtraction, multiplication, and division problems. Many educators differentiate between *estimation* and *approximation*. In this book, we have chosen to use the term *estimation* to cover both meanings. Those wishing to help their students learn both terms are encouraged to do so.

- Problem solving with mathematics is enhanced by the calculator. Some students have been dissuaded from attacking particular types of problems because of the length of the computations involved. The calculator frees these students to con-centrate on what information is required to solve a problem, what steps and operations are involved, and what answers are reasonable. *Calculator Math Levels D-E*, in particular, demonstrate how both everyday and more intricate mathematical problems (too cumbersome for a paper and pencil solution) can be handled easily with the aid of a calculator.

- Understanding fractions can also be enhanced by using a calculator. It can be used to develop the concept of a fraction and the relationship between common and decimal fractions. Calculator algorithms can be developed for operations with fractions. It should be noted that in spite of emphasis on the metric system and the increased emphasis on decimal fractions, common fractions have not disap-peared entirely (nor should they). Not only is the concept of $\frac{1}{3}$ much easier to grasp than $0.\overline{3}$, but students in the intermediate grades must be prepared to deal with algebra in the form $\frac{3}{5} + \frac{5}{4}$. Fractions also provide opportunities for students to think their way through various calculator algorithms. *Calculator Math Levels D-E* contain many activities that use common and decimal fractions. A series of activities is included to help students perform operations, such as $\frac{3}{4} + \frac{5}{8}$ on the calculator.

- Detecting and identifying patterns is the essence of inductive reasoning. The calculator can be a "number laboratory" where students perform a series of numerical experiments, develop hypotheses, and check conclusions by further experimentation. In the past, these types of exercises were impossible due to the drudgery of the required computations. Activities on patterns in all five *Calculator Math* books provide opportunities for students and teachers to engage in this type of experimentation.

- Teachers know that games, tricks, and puzzles help motivate students. They can be used to drill facts, expand concepts, and provide opportunities for discovery. Therefore, each *Calculator Math* book contains a section of games and similar activities for individuals, small groups, or entire classes.

The *Calculator Math* books have been created to make connections between the calculator's capabilities, learning mathematical concepts, and the application of those concepts to realistic problems. Each activity sheet can be duplicated in multiple copies with minimal expense. The teacher's guide and skill-and-topic annotations on the activity sheets help connect the activities to the mathematics curriculum. Many of the suggested activities use similar materials provided by the teacher or invented by the students. We urge teachers to build even more activities for their classes. They will enrich their mathematics programs while helping students productively use one of the technological marvels of the twentieth century.

The Authors

Contents

Content Lessons

Problem Solving

Answer Key

Activities Overview

Activity Category	Calculator Math Level A	Calculator Math Level B	Calculator Math Level C	Calculator Math Level D	Calculator Math Level E
About the Calculator	17	17-22	19-27		19-23
Counting	18-21				
Addition up to 10	22-25				
Subtraction up to 10	26-29				
Place Value	30-31				
Addition & Subtraction	32-44				
Money	45-51				
Multiplication		23-32			
Division		33-37			
Estimation	52-53	38-52	28-48	19-29	24-26
Games	54-79	53-65	52-61	30-40	27-34
Fractions			49-51	41-45	35-39
Patterns			62-64	47-49	40-50
Content Lessons		66-70		50-55	51-56
Problem Solving		71-72	65-72	56-72	57-71

Teacher's Guide

Recommendations for Calculator Purchases

To many people, a calculator is a calculator. However, there are great differences between the various brands and models of calculators. These differences include the type of logic employed (which dictates the order in which keys must be struck), available functions (%, √, and so on), display size, automatic/manual constant, floating/fixed decimal point, automatic display shut-down, size, spacing, key arrangement, sturdiness of case, durability, and power supply.

Selection of a particular model depends on the grade level of the students who will be using the machines and the purpose of the program. Features that are appropriate for calculators intended for elementary/intermediate school students include sturdiness, algebraic mode (natural order arithmetic), floating decimal point, 8-digit display, and automatic constant. Batteries are a frequent cause of breakdown, so choosing calculators equipped with small solar panels that gather energy from overhead lights are most suitable. Due to the large number of variations among calculators, it is desirable for all students in the elementary classroom to use the same model.

Several manufacturers produce calculators with transparent displays for use on overhead projectors. Students can watch examples step-by-step or perform demonstrations for their classmates. The model selected should have features similar to the calculators used by students at their desks.

Be careful when choosing calculators because some do not possess the automatic constant feature. This makes them useless for many important applications, such as "skip counting."

The Teacher's Guide provides direction for introducing the activities to students. The activity sheets are grouped by subject and are not necessarily intended to be done in order. Pick and choose among them, using those that fit best with your mathematics program.

If possible, arrange to have one calculator for each student. However, two or even three students per calculator is workable. It is crucial, however, that all students use the same model. Do not allow students to bring calculators from home unless they are the same as those used in class.

Calculators provide a fun and challenging asset to your mathematics program. Mastering skills in calculator use will not only help your students understand basic mathematics, but also provide an invaluable resource for future mathematics courses.

About the Calculator

THE COST OF MONEY I

Focus on . . .
   Introducing the % key
   Using the calculator effectively
   Developing consumer awareness

Extension Activity
   Discuss the differences in interest rates for borrowing money and investing money (such as in a savings account). Invite students to find the amount of interest they would pay to borrow $2000 at 9%, at 10%, at 12.5%, and at 18%. Then have them find the amount of interest they would earn in a savings account on $2000 at 4%, at 5%, at 5.5%, and at 6%. Point out the importance of shopping for the best interest rate whether borrowing or investing money.

THE COST OF MONEY II

Focus on . . .
Introducing the % key
Using the calculator effectively
Developing consumer awareness

Notes
Before calculating simple interest for more than a one-year period, check students' calculators. Some may have an automatic constant which helps to figure interest for periods greater than one year.

Extension Activity
Invite students to translate different per-month interest charges into yearly rates and calculate payments required for yearly or monthly periods.

THE STATE'S LITTLE BIT EXTRA

Focus on . . .
Using the % key
Understanding taxation

Notes
Students should be familiar with the percent key. They should also be aware that (in most states) sales tax is levied on certain categories of purchases.

Extension Activities
1. On any problem that deals with the purchase of goods, ask students to calculate sales tax. Invite them to make up problems for each other, using the proper tax rate for your locality.

2. Discuss the state's use of sales tax revenues.

MONEY, MONEY IN THE BANK I

Focus on . . .
Using the % key
Understanding compound interest
Using the calculator effectively

Notes
For the second problem, the calculator may be keyed in one of two ways:

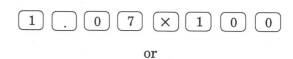

or

However, the first keying works only if the first number entered is the multiplicative constant. Students who have calculators operating with the second number as the constant should key the number 100 first, then 1.07. This sequence is shown in "Money, Money in the Bank II" on page 23, problem 1, method B.

Provide students with additional answers in the series and ask them to work out the keying sequence that produces those answers. Many students find this work difficult, so a slower pace may be required.

Extension Activity
Discuss the surprising speed with which compound interest adds up.

MONEY, MONEY IN THE BANK II

Focus on . . .
Using the % key
Understanding compound interest

Notes
Method B will not work as shown for calculators that operate with the first number entered as the multiplicative constant. However, most students are able to discover the keying sequence required for such calculators. Ask your students to estimate the first several answers for method B before using the calculator, so answers from inappropriate keying sequences will be spotted quickly.

Estimation

BERMUDA TRIANGLES

Focus on . . .
Estimating in multiplication
Conceptualizing limits

Notes
This exercise provides the opportunity for students to develop an intuitive concept of limits.

Extension Activity

Students can be challenged to work out the rule for deciding which triangles disappear with the fewest operations.

ALL-STAR ESTIMATING

Focus on . . .
Rounding with decimals
Estimating in multiplication

Notes
Students must understand significant digits and be able to round decimal fractions.

DIVIDE AND FIGURE

Focus on . . .
Estimating in division
Rounding in division

Notes
Students may be tempted to resort to their calculators before completing their estimations. Emphasize that the calculator is to be used only for checking estimated answers.

Games

FACTOR FINESSE

Focus on . . .
Practicing multiplication and division facts
Factoring

Notes
Students should understand the concept of factors.

Extension Activities
1. Start each round with a 3-digit number in the display.
2. Use a spinner with large numbers (15, 18, 22, 25, 33, 40, 45, 75).
3. Restrict players to adding or subtracting a number adjacent (on the calculator) to the number spun. (If, for example, 57 was in the display and Player B spun 6, then he or she has to choose among

2, 3, 5, 8, or 9.) There is no restriction if 10, 11, or 12 is spun. Note that in this last variation there is no solution for numbers, such as 65 and 70 if the call is for a multiple of 9. (No solution exists for numbers equivalent to 2 or 7, modulus 9.)

NAME YOUR NUMBERS

Focus on . . .
Estimating in multiplication and division

Notes
Players should alternate in choosing destination numbers.

"GET MEAN"

Focus on . . .
Collecting data
Estimating an average

Notes
Students should know how to calculate an average.

Extension Activity
Students can order the values entered to make a frequency distribution by writing them down at the same time they are keyed into the calculator. Then they can identify the median weight, the mode, and the range. The data could also be used to make a bar graph.

RIGHT ON

Focus on . . .
Estimating a factor with precision
Multiplying with decimal fractions

Notes
Some calculators may not operate with the first number entered as the multiplicative constant, so the keying sequence shown will not work. Newer calculators are usually capable of storing the starting number in memory, using the Memory Recall key for retrieval on each try. With other calculators, the starting number will have to be re-keyed for each try.

ROOT OF THE PROBLEM

Focus on . . .
Estimating in multiplication and division
Finding square roots

Notes
Students should be familiar with the concept of square roots before attempting this game. Students can be challenged to find different ways of checking their estimates using the calculator.

ANIMAL, VEGETABLE, OR NUMERAL?

Focus on . . .
Gathering data
Using factors and multiples
Developing problem-solving strategies

Notes
Groups of four or five students may work best for this game. Help students focus on the types of questions that can be used, even though these are suggested in the example.

Fractions

A DECIMAL BY ANOTHER NAME

Focus on . . .
Converting decimals to fractions
Working with equivalent fractions

Notes
Some classes may benefit from having more examples than those on the activity sheet. You may want to move through this activity step-by-step with the entire class, adding additional examples, if necessary.

IT'S ALL EQUAL

Focus on . . .
Converting fractions to decimals
Working with equivalent fractions

Notes
The correct method of changing $\frac{3}{5}$ to $\frac{15}{16}$ is to change $\frac{3}{5}$ to a decimal and then change the

decimal to a fraction with the denominator of 25. The keying sequence is:

This can be shown algebraically as:
$$\frac{3}{5} = \frac{x}{25}$$
$$\frac{3}{5} \times 25 = \frac{x}{25} \times 25$$
$$\boxed{3 \div 5 \times 25} = x$$

CALCULATING FRACTIONS I AND II

Focus on . . .
Adding and subtracting common fractions
Using the calculator effectively
Working with the distributive property
Working with calculator algorithms

Notes
Students should work through Exercises A, B, and C without using their calculators. Present the following mini-lesson after students have completed Exercise C.

1. Invite students to complete Exercise C, problem 1 by changing the fractions to decimals and then adding, using only the calculator. It may seem possible to solve problem 1 this way:

   Ask students to try this method and write down the answer. They should repeat the same kind of keying sequence for problem 2. Ask students to compare these answers with those obtained without the calculator.

2. Examine the problems with students. Explain that although

   appears to be a correct string of operations, the calculator operates on all preceding results as it goes along. The final keying (divide by 8) tells the machine to divide all its work up to that point by 8, even though the operator's intent was only that 7 be divided by 8.

3. Students can add a compensating step: Multiply $3 \div 4$ by 8 in advance, then

divide by 8 later on—the two operations will "undo" each other and the correct answer will be obtained from the calculator. On paper it would look like:

$$[(3 \div 4) \times 8) + 7] \div 8$$

instead of:

$$(3 \div 4) + (7 \div 8)$$

Invite students to try Exercise C, problem 2 for practice. They should punch in:

$$\boxed{1} \div \boxed{2} \times \boxed{1} \boxed{6} + \boxed{7}$$
$$\div \boxed{1} \boxed{6}$$

The correct answer is 0.9375.

4. Invite students to complete Exercise D on their calculators using the compensating step.

5. "Calculating Fractions II" on page 38 is an extension of "Calculating Fractions I." It uses the compensating step described in this section.

FAST FRACTIONS

Focus on . . .
Using the calculator effectively
Multiplying fractions
Working with calculator algorithms

Notes
Before proceeding with Exercise B, the following mini-lesson should be presented. Invite students to find $\frac{3}{4} \times 7$ on their calculators. There are four ways to do this:

a. $3 \div 4 \times 7 = 5.25$
b. $7 \div 4 \times 3 = 5.25$
c. $3 \times 7 \div 4 = 5.25$
d. $7 \times 3 \div 4 = 5.25$

Methods c and d have the same results on all calculators. However, under special circumstances, a may have a different result than b and b may have a different result than c. This is due to the calculator's habit of cutting off decimals when numbers exceed storage capacity. The technical term for this is *truncation*.

Patterns

PATTERN DISCOVERY

Focus on . . .
Detecting and completing patterns
Drawing conclusions

Notes
To complete problem 2, students must understand operations with negative numbers. Discuss the results of problems 1b, 1c, and 3. Point out that in the array with ten numbers in a row, products differ by 10; in the array with six numbers in a row, products differ by 6. In the array with ten numbers, the subtraction answers are 9 and 11 (the counting numbers before and after 10). The result with six numbers is similar.

Extension Activity
Challenge students to change the array to rows of eight numbers, rows of seven numbers, and so on, and see if they can discover whether the patterns hold. Other arrays may be made using only even numbers, negative numbers, or fractions. Encourage students to experiment with various arrays.

BE A NUMBER DETECTIVE I

Focus on . . .
Detecting and completing patterns

Notes
Some students may be unable to detect a pattern after three items. Encourage them to try the first prediction, using the calculator before making a prediction about the remaining items.

BE A NUMBER DETECTIVE II

Focus on . . .
Detecting and completing patterns
Explaining patterns
Squaring and square roots

Notes

Previous experience with geoboards and pegboards is very helpful.

The squares of dots show geometric justification for an algebraic sum. By dividing the squares as shown, each section represents one of the terms in the sum, while the square itself represents the sum. The length of the side of the square equals the number of terms. Therefore, (the number of terms)^2 equals the sum. For example, the sum $1 + 3 + 5 + 7 + 9 + 11 + 13 + 15$ has eight terms. Thus, $1 + 3 + 5 + 7 + 9 + 11 + 13 + 15 = 8^2 = 64$.

Extension Activity

The above notes provide the basis for finding a formula for the sum $1 + 3 + 5 + \ldots + n$. Students need only find a way to express the number of terms.

Answer: $\dfrac{(1 + n)^2}{2} = \text{sum}$

BE A SQUARE DETECTIVE

Focus on . . .
Detecting and explaining patterns
Squaring and square roots

Notes

Squared paper is helpful for this activity. Turning the paper to a 45° angle helps students arrange dots in a symmetrical pattern.

THE THREE-ANGLE DETECTIVE

Focus on . . .
Detecting and completing patterns
Explaining patterns
Squaring and square roots

Notes

As with "Be a Square Detective," squared paper is helpful for this activity.

PATTERN POWER

Focus on . . .
Detecting and explaining patterns
Understanding number properties
Developing algebraic reasoning

Extension Activity

After they have completed the activity sheet, invite students to find and explain some patterns of their own.

MORE PATTERN POWER

Focus on . . .
Detecting and explaining patterns
Understanding number properties
Developing algebraic reasoning

Extension Activity

After students have explained the patterns, invite them to choose a number that can be multiplied by any 2-digit number to make those two digits repeat several times. To do this, they can compare their work on problems 1 and 2 to that on problem 3. They can also create a repeating number, such as 434343 on the calculator display and divide by the two digits that repeat (in this case, 43). *Answer*: 10101 or 1010101

Have students factor the number to write a problem similar to problem 1.

SUPER PATTERN POWER

Focus on . . .
Detecting and explaining patterns
Understanding number properties
Developing algebraic reasoning

Extension Activity

After they have completed the activity sheet, invite students to find some patterns of their own and challenge other students to explain them.

A LITTLE BIT CLOSER

Focus on . . .
Detecting patterns
Conceptualizing limits

Notes

Introduce the phrase "the sequence approaches 1" or "the sequence tends to 1" to describe what is happening.

HOW CLOSE CAN YOU GET?

Focus on . . .
Detecting patterns
Conceptualizing limits
Understanding convergent sequence

Notes
Again introduce the phrase "the sequence approaches 1" or "the sequence tends to 1 (or another number)" as a description of the pattern being observed.

Extension Activity
Show students how to write the sequence in problem 1 in general form.

$$\frac{n+1}{n}, \text{ where } n = 1, 2, 3, \ldots$$

Invite them to write their answers for problems 5 and 6 in general form.
Possible answers:

5. $\dfrac{1}{n+1}$, where $n = 1, 2, 3, \ldots$

6. $\dfrac{n}{2n+1}$, where $n = 1, 2, 3, \ldots$

PAPER FOLDING CHALLENGE

Focus on . . .
Detecting patterns
Developing mathematical reasoning

Notes
Each student will need several sheets of paper. Encourage them to discover a pattern rather than counting parts and creases.

Extension Activity
Invite students to write formulas for the values in the tables.
1. Number of parts = $p + 1$, where $p =$ number of points.
2. Number of parts = 2^n, where $n =$ number of times folded; number of creases = $2^n - 1$, where $n =$ number of times folded.
3. Number of parts = 2^n, where $n =$ number of times folded; number of crease lines = n, where $n =$ number of times folded.

Content Lessons

MULTIPLICATION TRICK

Focus on . . .
Mental arithmetic
Finding patterns

Notes
Make sure students are aware of the conditions needed to make the "trick" work. It is useful for estimating square roots (e.g., to find the square root of 1369, consider 30×30, then 40×40, so the square root is between 30 and 40. Using this trick, $35 \times 35 = 1225$, so the square root is between 35 and 40).

Extension Activity
Students ready for a challenge could learn the trick for:

$$26 \times 86 = 22\ \ 36$$

$$22 = 2 \times 8 + 6 \qquad\qquad 36 = 6 \times 6$$

22 = first digit $\times$ first digit + last digit   36 = last digit $\times$ last digit

REMAINDERS AND THE CALCULATOR I

Focus on . . .
Developing calculator algorithms
Developing mathematical reasoning
Reviewing inverse operations

Notes
Allow students some "tinker time" to find an algorithm for determining the whole remainder from the decimal quotient. Ask them to find the elements that must be used in the longhand decimal problems if they are to compute the remainder from the decimal quotient. Present more examples, if necessary.

REMAINDERS AND THE CALCULATOR II

Focus on . . .
Developing calculator algorithms
Developing mathematical reasoning
Reviewing inverse operations

Notes

If needed, help students with the sequence shown for problem 2 by going through it with them on the calculator. Check answers to problem 3 to make sure students have consistently followed the proper sequence of operations.

REMAINDERS AND THE CALCULATOR III

Focus on . . .
Developing calculator algorithms
Developing mathematical reasoning
Reviewing inverse operations

Notes

Invite students to complete problems 1 through 4. Discuss what happens inside a calculator when it is presented with a problem, such as $(1 \div 3) \times 3$ and why the answer is 0.9999999 instead of 1. The process is called *truncation*. Better and more expensive calculators give the answer as 1.

Problems 1 and 3 are the same. Which answers do your students think are correct? Most calculators simply negate all digits after those to the right of the display. The answer on the machine is, therefore, a little bit "wrong." When that answer is multiplied by 3, the machine shows 0.9999999. The correct answer is 1, but the calculator's answer is very, very close. Remind students that when the calculator shows 0.9999999, it usually means 1.

GOING IN CIRCLES I

Focus on . . .
Discovering the relationship between circumference and diameter
Gathering data
Placing results in tabular form

Notes
1. Collect a variety of circular objects, such as wheels, discs, cans, bottles, Frisbees, or plates. Provide rulers, cloth tape, and pocket calculators.
2. Divide the class into pairs.
3. Invite students to measure the circumference and diameter of a variety of objects and record their findings in the table.
4. Using their calculators, students should complete the fourth column on the activity sheet (circumference ÷ diameter).
5. Discuss the similarity of the answers in column 4. Ask students to compute their averages for column 4. Then, compute the class average for column 4.
6. Discuss the meaning of π and ask students for their definitions.

Extension Activity

Use π in a variety of ways. For example, if a bicycle tire has a diameter of 70 cm, how far will it roll in one revolution? In 10 revolutions? In 100 revolutions? How many revolutions would be required to go around the world (circumference of the earth is approximately 40,000 km).

CHESS MASTER

Focus on . . .
Exponents

Notes

This activity presents a good opportunity to introduce students to exponential notation as a form of "shorthand." Students should develop an appreciation for the quick growth of exponential functions.

Extension Activity

Deal with the *sum* of all the grains owed, e.g., $2^{64} - 1$ (more than all the rice in the world). *Hint*: Use patterns.

Problem Solving

BEST BUYS

Focus on . . .
Working with ratio
Developing consumer awareness
Using the calculator judiciously

Notes

This may be a good time to discuss economic concepts, such as price competition, loss leaders, and the costs and benefits of advertising. A chart of the distances between major markets clarify why it is often uneconomical to save by finding the best buys wherever they may be located.

ONE OF EVERYTHING

Focus on . . .
Gathering data
Finding Averages
Estimation

Notes
Bring some catalogs to class and tear out pages to distribute to students.

Extension Activity
Discuss the strength and weakness of this method and extend it to opinion polls.

BATTER UP!

Focus on . . .
Finding and evaluating averages
Discerning the basis for an average

Notes
The criteria for answers to questions 1 and 2 can be discussed. Why, for instance, is Brown better to have on your team than Kolinski? The definition of a "batting average" should prelude averaging individual averages to get the team average. Invite students to compute the "average of the averages" and compare this answer to the team average. Ask them to explain why the average of the averages is lower. (The higher-average players are at bat proportionately more of the time, so their efforts raise the overall average. An average of the individual averages would err on the low side.)

IF THE SHOE FITS

Focus on . . .
Gathering data
Finding averages and ratios

Extension Activity
Challenge students to find other common items with similar easily identifiable components (e.g., shirt buttons) and work out assumptions and operations for calculating national totals.

FASTER THAN A SPEEDING SNAIL

Focus on . . .
Calculating ratios
Constructing graphs
Using constants

Notes
As students arrange the animals in order of speed (problem 1), they should write the results in the spaces to the left of the bar graph. Students should be aware that ratios can be expressed as decimals (e.g., $63 \div 45 = 1.40$). The most efficient method of computing ratio is to program the calculator constant to divide by 45 by keying:

SODA POP CHALLENGE

Focus on . . .
Gathering data
Finding averages and ratios
Developing consumer awareness
Reading and constructing tables

Extension Activity
Students can research the cost of various components of a year's supply of soda pop (sugar, water, flavoring, cans, and so on).

THINKING THROUGH THE PROBLEM

Focus on . . .
Analyzing problems

Notes
Be certain students know about leap years. These problems provide opportunities for estimation practice.

A DAY IN YOUR LIFE

Focus on . . .
    Gathering data
    Finding averages and percentages
    Reading and constructing tables

Extension Activity
    When completed, these tables are a good basis for constructing circle graphs.

MONEY MATTERS

Focus on . . .
    Collecting data
    Finding the mass of an object
    Conceptualizing limits
    Finding rates

Notes
    For the first problem, students will need to find out the current cost of a pack of commonly smoked cigarettes.
    For the second problem, they'll need an accurate scale and a number of coins.

Extension Activities
1. Students can compute how many bicycles, pairs of jeans, movies, or how much food could be purchased with money saved by not smoking for x number of years.
2. Invite students to find out how much they would be worth if they were worth their weight in pennies, dimes, nickels, or quarters.

GOING IN CIRCLES II

Focus on . . .
    Working with pi
    Working with ratios
    Finding rates of speed

Notes
    Have students use $355 \div 113$ to compute π to six significant figures.

Extension Activity
    Students can create similar problems for each other based on catalog sources, such as the *Guinness Book of World Records*.

BURGER BUSINESS

Focus on . . .
    Working with large numbers
    Working with ratios

Notes
    Useful metrics for this activity are:

1000 milliliters = 1 liter or, in volume terms, 1 cubic decimeter
    1 milliliter = 1 cubic centimeter
    1000 mL = 1 L
    1 mL = 1 cc

HUMMINGBIRD TRIVIA

Focus on . . .
    Integration with science
    Reading carefully for information
    Problem solving

Notes
    Answers will be in a range of values.
    These problems provide estimation opportunities. Students should estimate answers to see if actual calculations are reasonable.

Extension Activity
    Similar problems can be written about ants, bees, butterflies, and so on. Invite students to research other interesting facts about different creatures from which problems can be created.

FOR CALCULATING EXPERTS

Focus on . . .
    Advanced place value applications
    Problem solving

Notes
    These activities work well with small groups.
    To complete exercises, such as problem 3, think about place value: 8 and 7 in the thousands' column, 6 and 5 in the hundreds' column, 4 and 3 in the tens' column, and 2 and 1 in the ones' column. Students should form two numbers that are as close together as possible.

FRIENDS IN NUMBERS

Focus on . . .
Developing algebraic reasoning

Notes
During discussion, students may be able to see similarities between the two situations. A handshake between two people corresponds to giving each other a present. There will be twice as many presents as handshakes.

Name _____

The Cost of Money I

Simple interest—how much you pay.

Work through the following example.

Example

Deposit or Loan (Principal): $100

Interest Rate: 8%

Interest after 1 year = _____

Total owing after 1 year = _____

Solution

8% of $100 = 0.08 × $100 = $8

Interest = $8

Total owing = $100 (principal) + $8 (interest)

= $108

Look at the example. Your calculator can perform this type of operation.

Punch in [1] [0] [0] [+] [8] [%]. The display shows "8." This is the interest. Push [=].
The display shows "108." This is the total (principal + interest). Try the example again.

It is possible to find the total (principal + interest) in one step without using the [%] key.
For the example, the steps would be: [1] [0] [0] [×] [1] [.] [0] [8] [=]

100% (principal) + 8% (interest)

The display would read "108."
By subtracting the principal (100), you can find the interest (108 − 100 = 8).

1. Principal: $250

Interest Rate: 9%

Interest: $ _22.50_

Total owing (after 1year): _$272.50_

2. Find the value after 1 year of:

$87.49 invested at 9%: _95.8641_

$2645 invested at 12%: _2962.4_

3.

Principal	Rate	Interest	Total After 1 Year
$460.00	4%	18.4	478.4
$625.49	9%	6.85	681.74
$4000.00	11%	440	4440
$256.33	7%	17.94	274.87
$5847.00	9.5%	555.47	6402.47

Introducing the % key
Using the calculator effectively
Developing consumer awareness

Calculator Math Level E © 1995 Fearon Teacher Aids

The Cost of Money II
Calculate more simple interest.

Money is often borrowed or deposited for longer periods of time. In these cases, simple interest is computed on the original amount (the principal) every year.

Example
Principal: $300
Interest Rate: 6%
Loan Period: 4 years
Interest per year: _____
Interest for 4 years: _____
Interest + principal: _____

Solution
Interest for 1 year $= \$300 \times 0.06$
$= \$18$
Interest for 4 years $= \$18 \times 4$
$= \$72$
Total $= \$300 + \$72$
$= \$372$

Fast Method
Push: [3] [0] [0] [+] [6] [%] [=] [=] [=] [=]
4 years

1. Interest Rate: 14%
Period: 2 years
Total Payable: _____   **$867.99**

2. Interest Rate: 7%
Period: 4 years
Total after 4 years: _____   **$2469.00 (savings account)**

3.

Principal	Rate	Period	Interest	Total Payable
$420.25	12%	3 years	151.29	571.54
$1200.72	9.5%	5 years	570.34	1771.04
$1935.72	14%	15 years	4065.01	6000.73
$318.75	10%	12 years	382.5	701.25
$100.00	18%	50 years	900	1000

Introducing the % key
Using the calculator effectively
Developing consumer awareness

Calculator Math Level E © 1995 Fearon Teacher Aids

Name _____

The State's Little Bit Extra

Figure sales tax.

Exercise 1

Assuming a sales tax of 7%, find the total cost for articles priced as follows:

Cost	Cost + Sales Tax
$7.00	$7.49
$12.00	$12.84
$8.00	$8.56
$2.00	$2.14
$4.70	$5.03
Total Bill	$36.06

Find the total cost without sales tax first. Then calculate the tax for that total amount.
Is the total bill any different? __NO__

This is an illustration of the distributive property.

Explain._____

Exercise 2

Assuming a sales tax of 6%, find the total cost for articles priced as follows:

Cost	Cost + Sales Tax
$5.00	$5.30
$4.80	$5.09
$2.44	$2.59
$7.30	$7.74
$5.60	$5.94
Total Bill	$26.66

Use your calculator to find the total cost and then add the sales tax.
Is there a difference? Explain.

Yes, because rounded equals
$26.65 (.1¢ off)

Which method of calculating the total bill is fairer? Why?

The adding with the tax
is more accurate and fairer

Money, Money in the Bank I
Understanding compound interest.

Joan's grandfather gave her $100 to open a savings account.
At the end of each year, the bank pays 6% interest and adds it to the account.
Complete the table to show how Joan's account increases.

Principal: $100   Interest Rate: 6%   Term: 5 years (compound interest)

	Principal $		Interest $		Total $
Year 1	100	+	100 × 0.06 = 6	=	100 + 6 = 106
Year 2	106	+	6.36	=	112.36
Year 3	112.36	+	6.74	=	119.10
Year 4	119.10	+	7.15	=	126.25
Year 5	126.25	+	7.575	=	133.83

Interest which is added to the account each year to form the principal for the following year is called
compound interest. What is the difference between simple interest and compound interest?
Compound adds every year, and simple depends on rate

Which is more? Compound Why? Compound is more likely to raise

Complete the table below.

Principal: $100   Rate: 7%   Term: 6 years

	Principal $		Principal + Interest (Total) $
Year 1	100	1 . 0 7 × 1 0 0 or 1 0 0 + 7 %	107
Year 2	107	107 × .07 + 107	114.49
Year 3	114.49	1.07 × 114.49	122.50
Year 4	122.50	1.07 × 122.50	131.08
Year 5	131.08	1.07 × 131.08	140.26
Year 6	140.26	1.07 × 140.26	150.08

Using the % key
Understanding compound interest
Using the calculator effectively

Calculator Math Level E © 1995 Fearon Teacher Aids

Name _____

Money, Money in the Bank II
How compound interest adds up.

1. Complete the table.

Principal: $100   Rate of Interest: 8%   Loan Period: 5 years

Years	Principal + Interest Method A
	 `1` `0` `0` `+` `8` `%`
	 `=` `=` `=` `=` `=`
		Principal + Interest Method B
		 `1` `0` `0` `×` `1` `.` `0` `8`
		 `=` `=` `=` `=` `=`

1	100 + 8% = 108	100 × 1.08 = 108
2	100 + 8% = = 116.64	100 × 1.08 = = 116.64
3	100 + 8% = = = 125.97	100 × 1.08 = = = 125.97
4	100 + 8% = = = = 136.05	100 × 1.08 = = = = 136.05
5	100 + 8% = = = = = 146.93	100 × 1.08 = = = = = 146.93

Discuss the differences between the two methods.

With method A, you're working with percents unlike method B, which is decimals.

2. Use the methods shown above to complete the table.

Principal	Rate	Period	Total (Simple Interest)	Total (Compound Interest)
$400	7%	2 years	456.00	457.96
$960	12%	3 years	1305.60	1348.73
$1435	15%	5 years	2511.25	2886.30
$2869	18%	7 years	6482.94	9139.12
$5000	10%	10 years	10,000	12,968.49

3. The family Mark baby-sat for was so pleased with his work that they paid him a 10% increase over the previous year's rate at each of his birthdays. Mark decided to make a career out of baby-sitting for this family. He sat for nieces and nephews, for the children's children, and finally for great-grandchildren. He started at age 12 for $1.00 per hour. At age 85, he was still sitting for the same family. What was his hourly rate by this time? ___730.10___

Bermuda Triangles
Which triangles will vanish?

The Bermuda Triangle is a mysterious section of the Caribbean Ocean near Bermuda.
It is said that many ships and airplanes traveling through the area have never been heard from again.

Below is a collection of triangles, some of which are "Bermuda" triangles.
A triangle is a "Bermuda" triangle if, when you go around it, multiplying the numbers together, the product (answer) gets smaller and smaller and seems to disappear (it approaches zero).

Use your estimation skills to select the Bermuda triangles and place an X on each one.
Check your answers with your calculator.

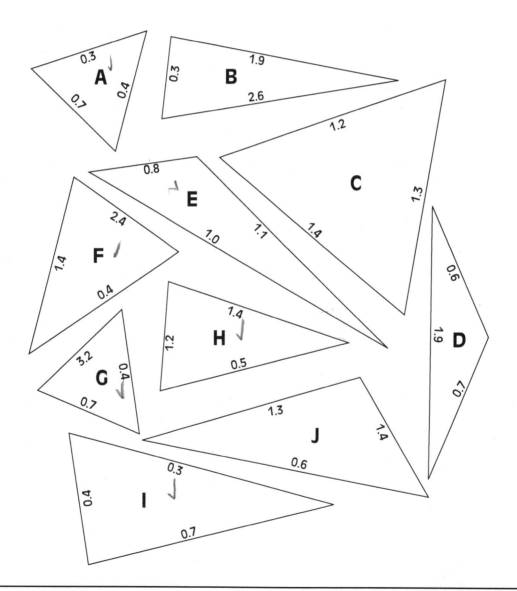

Calculator Math Level E © 1995 Fearon Teacher Aids

Estimating in multiplication
Conceptualizing limits

All-Star Estimating

Consider the decimals first.

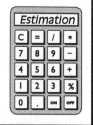

Estimate each product to at least two significant digits.
Check your estimates with your calculator.

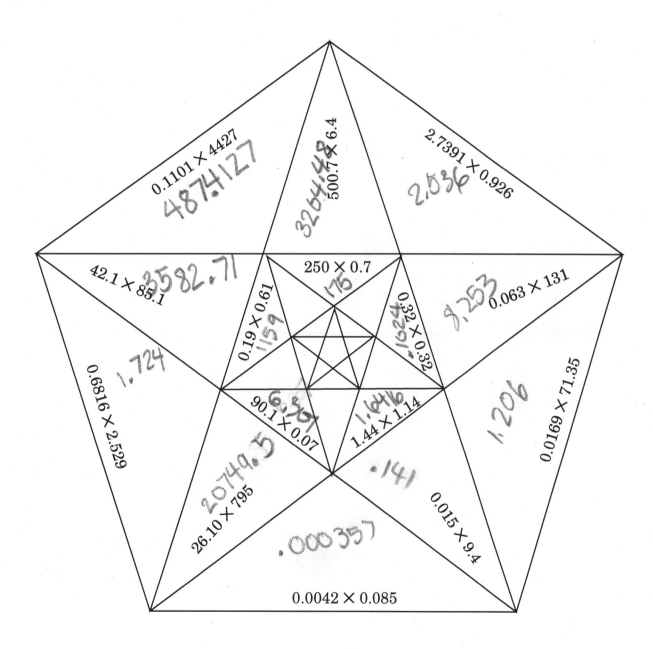

0.1101 × 4427 487.127

3264.48 × 6.4 500.7

2.7391 × 0.926 2.536

42.1 × 85.1 3582.71

250 × 0.7 175

0.063 × 131 8.253

0.19 × 0.61 .159

0.32 × 0.32 .1024

0.6816 × 2.529 1.724

90.1 × 0.07 6.307

1.44 × 1.14 1.6416

0.0169 × 71.35 1.206

26.10 × 795 20749.5

0.015 × 9.4 .141

0.0042 × 0.085 .000357

Divide and Figure
Rounding will help you.

Circle the answer which is the best estimate for each quotient.
Check your estimates with the calculator. The first one is done for you.

1.

a.	2822 ÷ 24	(100)	150	200
b.	1632 ÷ 47	(40)	70	100
c.	7965 ÷ 94	60	(80)	100
d.	1338 ÷ 82	10	(15)	20
e.	2248 ÷ 73	10	20	(30)

2.

f.	3777 ÷ 15	150	(200)	(250)
g.	6345 ÷ 62	50	(100)	150
h.	1066 ÷ 95	(10)	20	50
i.	2790 ÷ 98	10	(30)	50
j.	4008 ÷ 86	10	30	(50)

3.

k.	5054 ÷ 53	(50)	(100)	150
l.	8492 ÷ 21	200	300	(400)
m.	1426 ÷ 69	10	(20)	30
n.	2396 ÷ 84	10	20	(30)
o.	4026 ÷ 69	40	(60)	80

4.

p.	8425 ÷ 54	100	(150)	200
q.	1336 ÷ 35	(40)	60	80
r.	1909 ÷ 90	10	15	(20)
s.	7439 ÷ 32	(200)	300	400
t.	5388 ÷ 93	(50)	(75)	100

Estimating in division
Rounding in division

Calculator Math Level E © 1995 Fearon Teacher Aids

Factor Finesse
Multiply accurately and win!   (for 2 players)

Materials
Calculator
Spinner (page 28)
Score sheet (below)
Brass fastener
Scissors
Pencil

Instructions

1. Cut out the spinner and dial. Punch a hole through the center of the spinner face and the blunt end of the dial. Using a brass fastener, attach the dial to the spinner, prongs on the bottom. Secure with a piece of tape. Make sure and leave ¼" between dial and spinner face so that it will spin easily. You can duplicate spinners on various colored paper and laminate them for repeated use. (For a sturdier spinner, glue to a piece of cardboard.)

2. Player A displays a 2-digit number on the calculator (e.g., 59).

3. Player B spins the dial to find the "factor" (e.g., 11). Player B must then change the calculator display into a multiple of the number spun by adding or subtracting a 1-digit number (e.g., $59 - 4 = 55$).

4. If the display is already a required multiple, players may say, "Pass."

5. Player A may challenge Player B by checking whether the display is indeed one of the required multiples. If it is not, the challenger (Player A) scores a point; otherwise, the opponent (Player B) scores.

6. After each challenge, a new round starts. The winner is the player with the highest score after ten rounds.

ROUND	PLAYER A	PLAYER B
1		
2		
3		
4		
5		
6		
7		
8		
9		
10		
TOTAL		

Calculator Math Level E © 1995 Fearon Teacher Aids

Name _____

Name Your Numbers

Try some mental multiplication. (for 2 players)

Materials

Calculator
Score sheets (below)

Instructions

1. Player A selects a number (e.g., 500) as the destination. Both players write it on their score sheets.

2. Player B announces the starting number (e.g., 13). Both players record this number, also.

3. Each player now writes down a "multiplier" (a number to multiply by 13 to get 500). Decimals are permitted.

4. The player whose product is closer to 500 wins the round. (Check with the calculator.) The winner puts a check mark in the far right-hand column of his or her score sheet.

5. After each round, a new destination and a new starting number are chosen. The player who wins the most rounds out of ten is the champion.

Player A:				
Destination	Starting Number	Multiplier	Product	✓

Player B:				
Destination	Starting Number	Multiplier	Product	✓

"Get Mean"

Try this with as many players as possible. (for 3 to 20 players)

Materials

Calculator (display covered)
Score sheet (below)
Pencil

Instructions

1. Each player estimates and writes down the average weight, age, allowance, height, or some other statistic, for the group of players.

2. Player A enters his or her own weight, age, allowance, or height into the calculator.

3. Each player in turn adds his or her own figures.

4. Player A then divides the total by the number of players to find the mean, but does not announce it.

5. Each player announces his or her estimate and Player A declares the winner.

6. In case of a tie, both players may be given a chance to revise their estimates.

STATISTIC	MEAN	WINNER
Weight		
Age		
Allowance		
Height		
Waist		
Shoe Size		
Number in Family		

Right On

How accurately can you estimate? (for 2 players)

Materials
Calculator
Spinner (page 32)
Paper and pencil
Brass fastener
Scissors

Instructions

1. Cut out the spinner and dial. Punch a hole through the center of the spinner face and the blunt end of the dial. Using a brass fastener, attach the dial to the spinner, prongs on the bottom. Secure with a piece of tape. Make sure and leave ¼" between dial and spinner face so that it will spin easily. You can duplicate spinners on various colored paper and laminate them for repeated use. (For a sturdier spinner, glue to a piece of cardboard.)

2. Player A selects a number, such as 500, as the "target" and writes it down.

3. Player B spins the dial to get the "starter" number (e.g., 13) and stores it in the calculator as a multiplicative constant.

   (Press: 1 3 $\times$ $=$. Don't clear!)

4. Player A attempts to multiply the starter number by a decimal number (e.g., 38.1), resulting in 500.

5. Player B modifies Player A's choice to get even closer to the target (e.g., 38.2).

6. Player A then modifies Player B's choice, and so on.

7. The first player to reach the target number is the winner. (Anyone who goes over the target loses.)

8. Play a "Best of 7" series.

Estimating a factor with precision
Multiplying with decimal fractions

Calculator Math Level E © 1995 Fearon Teacher Aids

Root of the Problem

Guess square roots to win.   (for 2 players)

Materials

    Calculator
    Score sheet (below)
    Pencil

Instructions

1. While Player B looks away, Player A picks four
   consecutive numbers, multiplies them together, and adds 1.
   Player A then writes down this "target" number and shows it to Player B.

2. Player B has one try to estimate the square root of the target number.

3. If Player B is wrong, Player A takes a turn.

4. Players continue taking turns until one player finds the correct square root.

5. The player who finds the square root scores a point. Mark the winner on the
   score sheet.

6. Players take turns starting new rounds by creating a new target number.

7. The player who wins the most rounds out of ten is the winner.

ROUND	TARGET	WINNER (A or B)
1		
2		
3		
4		
5		
6		
7		
8		
9		
10		

Estimating in multiplication and division
Finding square roots

Animal, Vegetable, or Numeral?

Guess the hidden number.   (for 3 to 5 players)

Materials
Calculator
Paper and pencil

Instructions

1. Appoint one person as the game leader. He or she writes down a 1-, 2-, or 3-digit number on a piece of paper.

2. Player A tries to find the number by asking questions the leader can answer with a "Yes" or "No."

3. Whenever the leader answers, "No," it is the next player's turn to ask questions. A player who believes he or she knows the answer waits until his or her turn to present it.

4. The player who guesses the hidden number correctly wins.

5. The person to the left of the leader is the leader for the next round.

6. Players may use their calculators to help prepare questions. The game leader may use a calculator to help supply answers.

Example
Mary is game leader for the first game. She writes 324 on a piece of paper.

		Mary:
Penny:	Is the number 2 or more digits long?	Yes
	Is it 2 digits long?	No
Jim:	Is it 3 digits long?	Yes
	Is it divisible by 2?	Yes
	Is it divisible by 3?	Yes
	Is it divisible by 4?	Yes
	Is it divisible by 5?	No
Dale:	Is the number 756?	No
Kate:	Is it bigger than 200?	Yes
	Is it bigger than 500?	No
Penny:	Is it more than 300?	Yes
	Is it more than 400?	No
Jim:	Is the sum of the digits less than 10?	Yes
	Is the sum of the digits 9?	Yes
	Is the number 324?	Yes

Jim wins!

Gathering data
Using factors and multiples
Developing problem-solving strategies

Calculator Math Level E © 1995 Fearon Teacher Aids

A Decimal by Another Name

Convert decimals to fractions.

1. If you divide 312 by 4 and multiply your answer by 4, what do you think your answer will be? ___312___

   Try it on your calculator.

2. If you divide any counting number by 4 and multiply your answer by 4, what do you think your answer will be? __the counting number__

   Try it on your calculator. Write down five examples.

   a. $5 \div 4 \times 4 = 5$ b. $6 \div 4 \times 4 = 6$ c. $7 \div 4 \times 4 = 7$ d. $8 \div 4 \times 4 = 8$ e. $9 \div 4 \times 4 = 9$

3. A number is divided by 4. The answer is 1.25. What was the original number? ___5___

4. A number is divided by 8. The result is 0.375. What was the original number? ___3___

5. 0.375 equals what fraction? ___$\frac{3}{8}$___

6. A number is divided by 25. The result is 0.92. What was the number divided by 25?

   ___23___

7. The decimal fraction $0.92 = \frac{23}{25}$

8. Change the following decimal fractions to fractions with the required numerators.

   $0.3 = \frac{3}{10}$ $0.4 = \frac{2}{5}$ $0.75 = \frac{3}{4}$ $0.3125 = \frac{5}{16}$ $0.625 = \frac{5}{8}$

   $0.095 = \frac{19}{200}$ $0.6 = \frac{9}{15}$ $0.064 = \frac{8}{125}$ $0.2125 = \frac{17}{80}$ $0.75 = \frac{24}{32}$

   How can you show that $\frac{3}{4} = \frac{24}{32}$?

   (Think: $\frac{3}{4} = 0.75 = \frac{?}{32}$)

It's All Equal

Converting fractions made easy.

Use your calculator to convert $\frac{3}{5}$ to another fraction with a denominator of 25.

The answer should be: $\frac{3}{5} = \frac{15}{25}$.

Similarly, change the following fractions to equivalent forms.

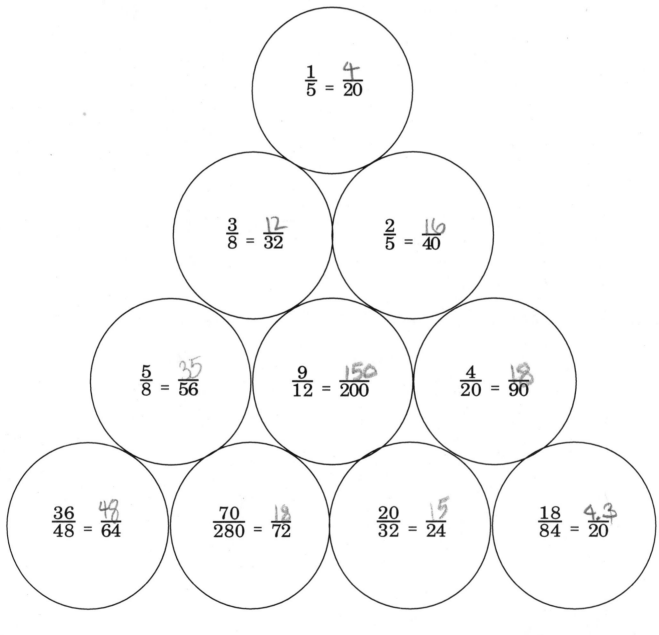

$\frac{1}{5} = \frac{4}{20}$

$\frac{3}{8} = \frac{12}{32}$

$\frac{2}{5} = \frac{16}{40}$

$\frac{5}{8} = \frac{35}{56}$

$\frac{9}{12} = \frac{150}{200}$

$\frac{4}{20} = \frac{18}{90}$

$\frac{36}{48} = \frac{48}{64}$

$\frac{70}{280} = \frac{18}{72}$

$\frac{20}{32} = \frac{15}{24}$

$\frac{18}{84} = \frac{4.3}{20}$

Converting fractions to decimals
Working with equivalent fractions

Calculator Math Level E © 1995 Fearon Teacher Aids

Calculating Fractions I
How does a calculator handle fractions?

Most calculators are not capable of showing common fractions on their displays.
Therefore, common fractions are usually changed to decimals.

Exercise A

Change these to decimal fractions.

$\frac{1}{2}$ = .5

$\frac{5}{8}$ = .625

$\frac{3}{4}$ = .75

How would you compute the decimal fraction
for $\frac{27}{45}$? 27÷45

Exercise B

Add these fractions, showing all your work.
Change your answer to a decimal fraction.

$\frac{2}{5}$ + $\frac{3}{4}$ = $\frac{2}{5} \times \frac{4}{4} = \frac{8}{20}$ $\frac{8}{20} + \frac{15}{20} =$

$\frac{8}{20} \times \frac{5}{5} = \frac{15}{20}$ $\frac{23}{20} = 1.15$

Your work should look like:

$\frac{2}{5} + \frac{3}{4} = \frac{2 \times 4}{5 \times 4} + \frac{3 \times 5}{4 \times 5}$

$= \frac{8}{20} + \frac{15}{20}$

$= \frac{23}{20}$

$= 1\frac{3}{20}$

$= 1\frac{15}{100}$

$= 1.15$

It's easier to change each fraction to a decimal
first, and then add.
For example:

$\frac{2}{5} + \frac{3}{4} = 0.4 + 0.75 = 1.15$

Exercise C

Add these fractions, showing all your work.

1. $\frac{3}{4}$ + $\frac{7}{8}$ = .75 + .875 = 1.625

2. $\frac{1}{2}$ + $\frac{7}{16}$ = .5 + .4375 = .9375

Your work should look like:

1. $\frac{3}{4} + \frac{7}{8} = 0.75 + 0.875 = 1.625$

2. $\frac{1}{2} + \frac{7}{16} = 0.5 + 0.4375 = 0.9375$

Exercise D

Add these fractions, showing all your work.

1. $\frac{9}{25}$ + $\frac{36}{64}$ = .36 + .5625 = .9225

2. $\frac{15}{24}$ + $\frac{35}{40}$ = .625 + .875 = 1.5

Adding and subtracting common fractions
Using the calculator effectively
Working with the distributive property
Working with calculator algorithms

Calculator Math Level E © 1995 Fearon Teacher Aids

37

Name _____

Calculating Fractions II

More on how the calculator handles fractions.

Calculator Math Level E © 1995 Fearon Teacher Aids

Exercise A

Add $\frac{1}{2} + \frac{7}{16}$ =

You should have punched in ⟨ 1 ⟩ ⟨ ÷ ⟩ ⟨ 2 ⟩ ⟨ × ⟩ ⟨ 1 ⟩ ⟨ 6 ⟩ ⟨ + ⟩ ⟨ 7 ⟩ ⟨ ÷ ⟩ ⟨ 1 ⟩ ⟨ 6 ⟩

Correct answer: 0.9375

Add these fractions, using your calculator.

1. $\frac{5}{8} + \frac{1}{4}$ = .875   2. $\frac{17}{20} + \frac{4}{5}$ = 1.65   3. $\frac{6}{10} + \frac{19}{40}$ = 1.075   4. $\frac{5}{16} + \frac{1}{2}$ = .8125

Exercise B

Example: $\frac{3}{4} - \frac{1}{2}$ = ⟨ 3 ⟩ ⟨ ÷ ⟩ ⟨ 4 ⟩ ⟨ × ⟩ ⟨ 2 ⟩ ⟨ − ⟩ ⟨ 1 ⟩ ⟨ ÷ ⟩ ⟨ 2 ⟩ = 0.25

Subtract these fractions, using your calculator.

1. $\frac{5}{8} - \frac{3}{10}$ = .325   2. $\frac{15}{16} - \frac{3}{4}$ = .1875   3. $\frac{7}{8} - \frac{13}{40}$ = .55   4. $\frac{9}{16} - \frac{1}{2}$ = .0625

Exercise C
Examples:

I. $\frac{3}{4} + \frac{1}{2} + 6$

⟨ 3 ⟩ ⟨ ÷ ⟩ ⟨ 4 ⟩ ⟨ × ⟩ ⟨ 2 ⟩ ⟨ + ⟩ ⟨ 1 ⟩ ⟨ ÷ ⟩ ⟨ 2 ⟩ ⟨ + ⟩ ⟨ 6 ⟩ = 7.25

II. $\frac{3}{4} + \frac{1}{2} + \frac{5}{8}$

⟨ 3 ⟩ ⟨ ÷ ⟩ ⟨ 4 ⟩ ⟨ × ⟩ ⟨ 2 ⟩ ⟨ + ⟩ ⟨ 1 ⟩ ⟨ ÷ ⟩ ⟨ 2 ⟩ ⟨ × ⟩ ⟨ 8 ⟩ ⟨ + ⟩ ⟨ 5 ⟩ ⟨ ÷ ⟩ ⟨ 8 ⟩ = 1.875

1. $\frac{3}{4} + \frac{7}{16} + \frac{11}{40}$ = 12.22   2. $\frac{1}{10} + \frac{7}{8} + \frac{5}{16}$ = .4875   3. $\frac{3}{8} + \frac{2}{5} - \frac{1}{2}$ = .275   4. $\frac{6}{8} - \frac{1}{16} - \frac{3}{20}$ = .5375

Adding and subtracting common fractions
Using the calculator effectively
Working with the distributive property
Working with calculator algorithms

Name _____

Fast Fractions

How you can help your calculator.

Exercise A

1. $\frac{3}{7} \times 4 = \frac{12}{7} = 1\frac{5}{7}$

2. $\frac{2}{5} \times 12 = \frac{24}{5} = 4\frac{4}{5}$

3. $5 \times \frac{2}{9} = \frac{10}{9} = 1\frac{1}{9}$

4. $8 \times \frac{4}{3} = \frac{32}{3} = 10\frac{2}{3}$

Multiply $\frac{7}{10} \times \frac{5}{8}$ on your calculator. Your answer should be 0.4375.
What is one way to perform this operation?

7	×	5	÷	10	÷	8

Exercise B

1. $\frac{5}{6} \times \frac{9}{10} =$ .75

2. $\frac{3}{4} \times \frac{5}{8} =$ .46875

3. $\frac{3}{8} \times \frac{7}{5} =$ .525

4. $\frac{4}{14} \times \frac{7}{4} =$ .5

5. $\frac{13}{29} \times \frac{5}{26} =$ .0862068

Exercise C

1. $\frac{5}{8} \times \frac{4}{6} \times \frac{9}{10} =$ .375

2. $\frac{7}{16} \times \frac{2}{5} \times \frac{5}{12} =$ .0729166

3. $\frac{5}{6} \times \frac{5}{8} \times \frac{33}{8} =$ 2.148437

4. $\frac{4}{15} \times \frac{5}{26} \times \frac{100}{3} =$ 1.7094016

Using the calculator effectively
Multiplying fractions
Working with calculator algorithms

39

Pattern Discovery

Discover your own pattern.

Consider the array below.

```
 1    2    3    4    5    6    7    8    9   10
⑪   ⑫   13   14   15   16   17   18   19   20
21   22   23   24   25   26   27   28   29   30
31   32   33  ㉞   ㉟   36   37   38   39   40
㊶   42   43  ㊹   ㊺   46  ㊼   48   49  ㊿
㉛   ㉜   53   54   55   56   57   58   59   60
61   62   63   64   65   66  ㉗   68   69  ㉘
71   72   73   74   75   76   77   78   79   80
81   82   83   84   85   86   87   88   89   90
91   92   93   94   95   96   97   98   99  100
```

1. Compare the pair 34, 45 with the pair 44, 35.

a. Add: $34 + 45 = \underline{79}$

$44 + 35 = \underline{79}$

What do you notice about the answers?

They're the same

Is that true for any two such pairs?

Yes

b. Subtract: $45 - 34 = \underline{11}$

$44 - 35 = \underline{9}$

How do the answers differ?

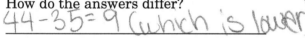
$44 - 35 = 9$ (which is lower)

Is that true for any two such pairs?

Yes

c. Multiply: $34 \times 45 = \underline{1530}$

$35 \times 44 = \underline{1540}$

How do the answers differ?

$34 \times 45 = 1530$

Is that true for any two such pairs?

Yes

2. Describe some of the patterns you found. Do they hold true if the array is extended to include negative numbers?

If you add 34 & 45 you'll get 79, same with 35+44, so if you turned them into neg, it still be 79 except negative.

3. What happens to your pattern if the array is changed as follows?

```
 1    2    3    4    5    6
 7    8    9   10   11   12
13   14   15   16   17   18
19   20   21   22   23   24
```

It will still have the same effect.

Detecting and completing patterns
Drawing conclusions

Calculator Math Level E © 1995 Fearon Teacher Aids

Be a Number Detective I
Can you predict the patterns?

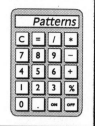

1. **Use your calculator:**

$1 \div 3 =$ _.33_

$10 \div 33 =$ _.3030303_

$100 \div 333 =$ _.3003003_

Predict:

$1000 \div$ _3333_ $=$ _.3003_

$10,000 \div$ _33333_ $=$ _.30003_

$100,000 \div$ _333333_ $=$ _.300003_

Check your guesses.

2. **Use your calculator:**

$1 \div 7 =$ _.1428571_

$2 \div 7 =$ _.285714_

$3 \div 7 =$ _.4285714_

Predict:

$4 \div 7 =$ _.5714285_

_5_ $\div 7 =$ _.7142857_

6 \div 7 $=$ _.857428_

Hint: Notice the order of the digits.

3. **Use your calculator:**

$1 \times 9 =$ _9_

$11 \times 99 =$ _1089_

$111 \times 999 =$ _110889_

$1111 \times 9999 =$ _11108889_

Predict:

$11,111 \times 99,999 =$ _1111088889_

$111,111 \times 999,999 =$ _1.11108889 11_

Be a Number Detective II
Discover more patterns.

Complete the pattern.

1	=	1	=	1^2
1 + 3	=	4	=	2^2
1 + 3 + 5	=	9	=	3^2
1 + 3 + 5 + 7	=	16	=	4^2
1 + 3 + 5 + 7 + 9	=	25	=	5^2
1 + 3 + 5 + 7 + 9 + 11	=	36	=	6^2
1 + 3 + 5 + 7 + 9 + 11 + 13	=	49	=	7^2
Guess: 1 + 3 + 5 . . . + 19	=	_____	=	_____

1.
To understand what is happening, count the number of dots in each section of the square.

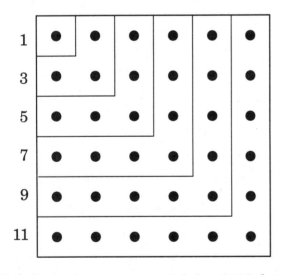

This figure is a square containing 6 × 6 dots.
Therefore, $1 + 3 + 5 + 7 + 9 + 11 = 6^2$.

2.
Complete the diagram below to illustrate the sum:

$$1 + 3 + 5 + 7 + 9 + 11 + 13 + 15$$

1
3
5
7
9
11
13
15

Write the corresponding number sentence.

Use your calculator to check whether $1 + 3 + 5 + 7 + . . . + 31$ is a perfect square.

Detecting and completing patterns
Explaining patterns
Squaring and square roots

Calculator Math Level E © 1995 Fearon Teacher Aids

Be a Square Detective
Showing squares with dot patterns.

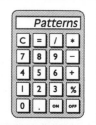

Complete the pattern.

$$
\begin{array}{rcl cl}
1 & = & 1 & = & 1^2 \\
1 + 2 + 1 & = & 4 & = & 2^2 \\
1 + 2 + 3 + 2 + 1 & = & 9 & = & 3^2 \\
1 + 2 + 3 + 4 + 3 + 2 + 1 & = & 16 & = & 4^2 \\
1 + 2 + 3 + 4 + 5 + 4 + 3 + 2 + 1 & = & 25 & = & 5^2 \\
1 + 2 + 3 + 4 + 5 + 6 + 5 + 4 + 3 + 2 + 1 & = & 36 & = & 6^2
\end{array}
$$

Now guess:

$1 + 2 + 3 + 4 + 5 + 6 + 7 + 8 + 9 + 10 + 9 + 8 + 7 + 6 + 5 + 4 + 3 + 2 + 1 = $ ___100___

$= $ _____

Use this dot pattern to explain what is happening.

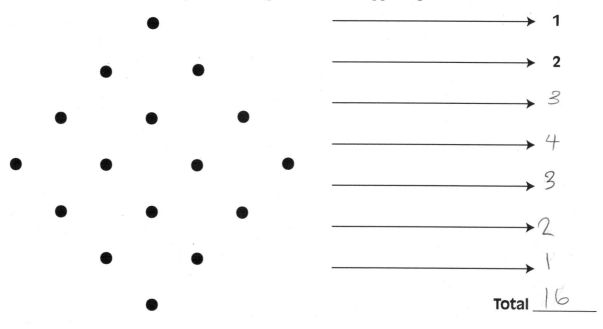

The figure is a square containing ___4___ × ___4___ dots.

Therefore, $1 + 2 + 3 + 4 + 3 + 2 + 1 = ($ ___4___ $)^2$.

Draw a similar dot diagram on the back of this sheet to explain why
$1 + 2 + 3 + 4 + 5 + 4 + 3 + 2 + 1 = 5^2$.

The Three-Angle Detective

Discover dot patterns for triangles.

1	=	1	=	4	=	2^2
1 + 2	=	3	=	9	=	3^2
1 + 2 + 3	=	6	=	16	=	4^2
1 + 2 + 3 + 4	=	10	=	25	=	5^2
1 + 2 + 3 + 4 + 5	=	15	=	36	=	6^2
1 + 2 + 3 + 4 + 5 + 6	=	21	=	49	=	7^2
1 + 2 + 3 + 4 + 5 + 6 + 7	=	28				

The numbers 1, 3, 6, 10, and so on, are called *triangular numbers*.
Look at the dot patterns to see why.

What happens when one triangular number is added to the next?
Explain, using the dot pattern below.

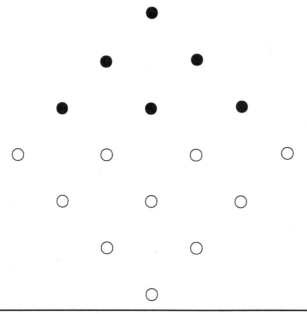

Detecting and completing patterns
Explaining patterns
Squaring and square roots

44

Calculator Math Level E © 1995 Fearon Teacher Aids

Pattern Power

Can you explain these patterns?

1.

6 ×	9	=	54
6 ×	99	=	594
6 ×	999	=	5994
6 ×	9999	=	59994
6 ×	99999	=	599994
6 ×	999999	=	5999994

2.

9 ×	6	=	54
9 ×	66	=	594
9 ×	666	=	5994
9 ×	6666	=	59994
9 ×	66666	=	599994
9 ×	666666	=	5999994

Compare your answers for exercises 1 and 2. Explain.

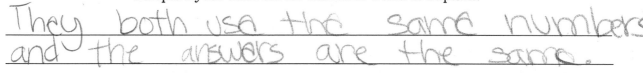

They both use the same numbers, and the answers are the same.

3.

4 ×	2	=	8
4 ×	22	=	88
4 ×	222	=	888
4 ×	2222	=	8888
4 ×	22222	=	88888
4 ×	222222	=	888888

4.

2 ×	4	=	8
2 ×	44	=	88
2 ×	444	=	888
2 ×	4444	=	8888
2 ×	44444	=	88888
2 ×	444444	=	888888

Compare your answers for exercises 3 and 4. Explain.

_____

_____

_____

5. Pick any two 1-digit numbers (e.g., 3 and 8).
Form a pattern similar to those in exercises 1-4.

3 × 8 =	8 × 3 =
3 × 88 =	8 × 33 =

Compare your answers and then try another example.

Detecting and explaining patterns
Understanding number properties
Developing algebraic reasoning

Name _____

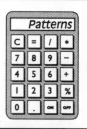

More Pattern Power

More pattern explorations.

1. Store any 1-digit number in your calculator.
Multiply by 3. Multiply by 37.
Compare your answer with the original number. Explain.

multiplying 3 & 37 tripled my number to 666. (original 6)

2. Store any 1-digit number in your calculator.
Multiply by 13. Multiply by 7. Multiply by 11. Multiply by 37. Multiply by 3.
Compare your answer with the starting number. Explain.

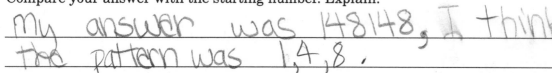

My answer was 148148, I think the pattern was 1,4,8.

3. Store any 3-digit number in your calculator.
Multiply by 13. Multiply by 7. Multiply by 11.
Compare your answer with your starting number. Explain.

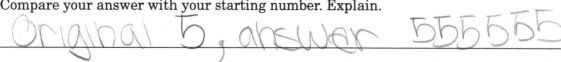

Original 5, answer 555555

4. Store any 1-digit number in your calculator.
Multiply by 16. Multiply by 43. Multiply by 1483.
Look for the pattern in your answer. Explain.

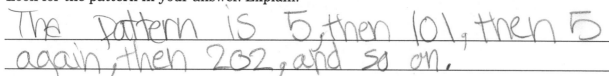

The pattern is 5, then 101, then 5 again, then 202, and so on.

Detecting and explaining patterns
Understanding number properties
Developing algebraic reasoning

Calculator Math Level E © 1995 Fearon Teacher Aids

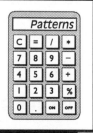

Super Pattern Power

Explain the patterns.

1.

$1 \times 7 \times 11 \times 13 =$ _1001_
$2 \times 7 \times 11 \times 13 =$ _2002_
$3 \times 7 \times 11 \times 13 =$ _3003_
$4 \times 7 \times 11 \times 13 =$ _4004_

Explain the pattern.

Add 1001 to the answer

2.

$1 \div 11 =$ _.0909_
$2 \div 11 =$ _.18181_
$3 \div 11 =$ _.27272_
$4 \div 11 =$ _.36363_
$5 \div 11 =$ _.45454_
$6 \div 11 =$ _.545454_

Explain the pattern.

The first number × 9.

3.

$12{,}345{,}679 \times 9 =$ _E1.11111_
$12{,}345{,}679 \times 18 =$ _E2.222_
$12{,}345{,}679 \times 27 =$ _E3.333_
$12{,}345{,}679 \times$ _36_ $=$ _E4.444_
_12345679_ $\times$ _45_ $=$ _E5.555_
_12345679_ $\times$ _54_ $=$ _E6.666_

Explain the pattern.

The whole number repeats in decimal

4.

$2 + 4$	$=$	6	$=$	2×3
$2 + 4 + 6$	$=$	12	$=$	3×4
$2 + 4 + 6 + 8$	$=$	_20_	$=$	_4×5_
$2 + 4 + 6 + 8 + 10$	$=$	_30_	$=$	_5×6_

Use the graphic below to explain why
$2 + 4 + 6 + 8 + 10 = 5 \times 6$.

The shaded parts are cut-offs, so the cut-off can fit into the unshade part form a square of 5x6.

			1	1	1
		1	2	2	2
		2	3	3	3
	1	3	4	4	4
	2	4	5	5	5

Detecting and explaining patterns
Understanding number properties
Developing algebraic reasoning

Calculator Math Level E © 1995 Fearon Teacher Aids

47

A Little Bit Closer

What is a convergent sequence?

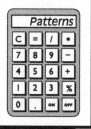

1. Use your calculator to find these decimal equivalents.

  a. $\frac{1}{2}$ = .5

  b. $\frac{2}{3}$ = .6̄

  c. $\frac{3}{4}$ = .75

  d. $\frac{4}{5}$ = .8

  e. $\frac{5}{6}$ = .83̄

  f. $\frac{6}{7}$ = .8571428

  g. $\frac{7}{8}$ = .875

Write the next three fractions in the sequence and their decimal equivalents.

  h. $\frac{8}{9}$ = .88888

  i. $\frac{9}{10}$ = .9

  j. $\frac{10}{11}$ = .909

2. Mark those values above on the number line.

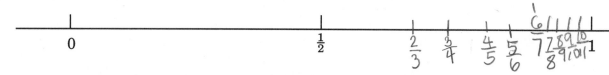

3. What do you notice when each term is compared to the next?

It the bottom, on to and the number up is on bottom

4. To what number are the sequential terms getting closer? 8, 9

How can you test that guess?

by dividing 8 by 9,

How Close Can You Get?

More about convergent sequences.

Patterns

Examine this sequence: $\frac{2}{1}, \frac{3}{2}, \frac{4}{3}, \frac{5}{4}, \ldots$

1. Use your calculator to find these decimal equivalents.

   a. $\frac{2}{1}$ = 2

   b. $\frac{3}{2}$ = 1.5

   c. $\frac{4}{3}$ = 1.33

   d. $\frac{5}{4}$ = 1.25

   e. $\frac{6}{5}$ = 1.2

   f. $\frac{7}{6}$ = 1.16

   g. $\frac{8}{7}$ = 1.1428

Find the next three terms in the sequence and their decimal equivalents.

   h. $\frac{9}{8}$ = 1.125

   i. $\frac{10}{9}$ = 1.1111

   j. $\frac{11}{10}$ = 1.1

2. Mark those values above on the number line.

$1\frac{10}{9}\ \frac{11}{10}\frac{12}{7}\ \frac{5}{4}\quad \frac{6}{5}\quad \frac{4}{3}\ \frac{9}{8}\ \frac{8}{7}\qquad 1\frac{1}{2}\qquad\qquad\qquad\qquad 2$

3. What do you notice when each term in the sequence is compared to the next?

They're smaller in number

4. To what number is the sequence getting closer? ___ 8.7 ___
This number is called the *sequence limit*.

5. Can you find a sequence that has a limit of 0? Check your guess with the calculator. What is the sequence?

_____

6. Can you find a sequence that has a limit of $\frac{1}{2}$? (Hint: The denominator may have to be at least twice as large as the numerator.) Check with your calculator. What is the sequence?

_____

Detecting patterns
Conceptualizing limits
Understanding convergent sequence

Paper Folding Challenge
Creases, pieces, lines, and numbers.

1. A point divides a line into two parts.

Two points divide a line into how many parts?

Complete the table on the right to show points and parts.

Number or Points	Number of Parts
1	2
2	3
3	4
4	5
6	6
82	83

2. Fold a sheet of paper in half. Fold the paper again in the same direction (see illustration). Into how many parts is the paper divided? Complete the table below.

Number of Times Folded	Number of Parts	Number of Creases
1	2	1
2	4	3
3	6	5
4	8	7
5	10	9
10	20	19
20	40	39

3. Fold a sheet of paper in half. Fold again in the other direction. Into how many parts is the paper divided? How many crease lines go all the way across the page? Complete the table below.

Number of Times Folded	Number of Parts	Number of Creases
1	2	1
2	4	2
3	8	3
4	16	4
5	32	5
6	64	6
20	1,046,576	20

Detecting patterns
Developing mathematical reasoning

Calculator Math Level E © 1995 Fearon Teacher Aids

Multiplication Trick

Amaze your friends.

$$\boxed{\begin{array}{c} 7 \times (7+1) \\ = \\ 7 \times 8 \end{array}} \Rightarrow \begin{array}{r} 74 \\ \times\ 76 \\ \hline 56\ 24 \end{array} \Leftarrow \boxed{4 \times 6}$$

This trick works only if . . .
- *the one's digits add up to 10, and*
- *the ten's digits are the same.*

1. Estimate these multiplication problems in your head, using the "trick." Write the answer in the second column. Check with your calculator and write that answer in the third column.

QUESTION	ANSWER BY ESTIMATION	ANSWER BY CALCULATOR	✔
25 × 25	625	625	✓
34 × 36	1224	1224	✓
78 × 72	5616	5616	✓
95 × 95	9025	9025	✓
47 × 43	2021	2021	✓
14 × 16	224	224	✓
61 × 69	4209	4209	✓
58 × 52	3016	3016	✓
45 × 45	2025	2025	✓
103 × 107	11021	11021	✓

2. Create five similar exercises, completing them in your head and then with the calculator. Work with a partner to see which way is faster.

___

Mental arithmetic
Finding patterns

Name _____ *Brian Nguyen* _____

Remainders and the Calculator I
What that decimal remainder means.

1. Complete these division problems in longhand. Leave a remainder.
The first one is done for you.

a. 4)30 → 7R2   **b.** 5)23 → 4R3   **c.** 8)46 → 5.R6   **d.** 4)38 → 9R2

2. Complete these division problems in longhand. Use decimals.
Check with your calculator. The first one is done for you.

a. 4)30.0 → 7.5   **b.** 5)23.0 → 4.6   **c.** 8)46.00 → 5.75   **d.** 4)38.0 → 9.5

Compare problems **1a** and **2a**.
Use the decimal quotient to find the remainder.

$$\begin{array}{r} 7.5 \\ \times\,4 \\ \hline 30.0 \end{array}$$

or

$$7.5 \times 4 = (7 + 0.5) \times 4 = (7 \times 4) + (0.5 \times 4)$$
$$= 28 + ②\ \text{Remainder}$$
$$= 30$$

Use your calculator to find the remainder from the decimal quotient.
Write down which buttons you push to check the remainders for problems **b**, **c**, and **d** above.

b. $4.6 \times 5 = 23.0$

c. $5.75 \times 8 = 46.00$

d. $9.5 \times 4 = 36.0$

Developing calculator algorithms
Developing mathematical reasoning
Reviewing inverse operations

Calculator Math Level E © 1995 Fearon Teacher Aids

Remainders and the Calculator II
The easy way to find decimal remainders.

1. Find the whole number remainder.

$$6\overline{)39} \quad \frac{6.5}{}$$

$$4\overline{)43} \quad \frac{10.75}{}$$

$$5\overline{)62} \quad \frac{12.4}{}$$

R = 3   R = 3   R = 2

384 ÷ 15 = 25.6. What whole number remainder does the 0.6 stand for? ___9___

2. Find a method for determining the whole number remainder without clearing the calculator.

434 ÷ 35   **Answer:** ___12.4___
Whole number part: ___12___
Fractional part: ___.4___
Whole number remainder: ___14___

Your steps should be:

[4] [3] [4] [÷] [3] [5] [=] ([12.4] [−] [1] [2]) [×] [3] [5] [=]
                                                Display

3. Find the quotient and remainder, using your calculator. The first one is done for you.

	Quotient	Remainder
17 ÷ 2	8	1
23 ÷ 4	5	3
184 ÷ 16	11	8
200 ÷ 10	20	0
163 ÷ 8	20	3
4403 ÷ 136	32	51
1239 ÷ 42	29	31
6734 ÷ 185	36	74

Developing calculator algorithms
Developing mathematical reasoning
Reviewing inverse operations

53

Calculator Math Level E © 1995 Fearon Teacher Aids

Remainders and the Calculator III

Test your skill with remainders.

1. Multiply. Work out longhand.

$\frac{1}{3} \times 3$ $\qquad$ $\frac{4}{9} \times 9$ $\qquad$ $\frac{2}{3} \times 6$

= _____1_____ $\qquad$ = _____4_____ $\qquad$ = _____4_____

2. Change to decimals.

$\frac{1}{3}$ = ___.$\overline{33}$___ $\qquad$ $\frac{4}{9}$ = ___.$\overline{4444}$___ $\qquad$ $\frac{2}{3}$ = ___.$\overline{666}$___

3. Repeat these problems, using your calculator.

$\frac{1}{3} \times 3$ $\qquad$ $\frac{4}{9} \times 9$ $\qquad$ $\frac{2}{3} \times 6$

= _____1_____ $\qquad$ = _____4_____ $\qquad$ = _____4_____

4. Compare the answers from the problems in exercises 1 and 3.
Which answers are correct?

_____

When the calculator displays 0.9999999, it usually means 1.

5. Find the quotient and whole number remainder for these division problems.

	Quotient	Remainder
$62 \div 3$	20	2
$73 \div 9$	8	1
$84 \div 13$	6	6
$127 \div 7$	18	1
$135 \div 19$	7	2
$236 \div 21$	11	5
$6087 \div 89$	68	25
$2111 \div 17$	124	3

Developing calculator algorithms
Developing mathematical reasoning
Reviewing inverse operations

Calculator Math Level E © 1995 Fearon Teacher Aids

Name _____

Going in Circles I
Make the pi discovery.

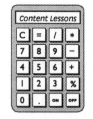

Materials
Variety of circular objects
(wheels, discs, cans, bottle tops, cardboard circles)
Measuring tape
Ruler
Calculator
Worksheet (below)
Pencil

Definitions
Circumference: The distance around the outside of a circle.
Diameter: The distance across a circle, passing through the center.

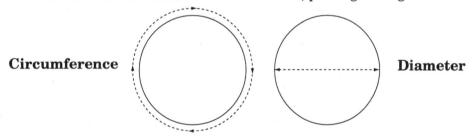

Instructions
Measure the circumference and diameter of a variety of circular objects.
Write your findings in the table below. Use your calculator to help you fill in the last column.

Object	Circumference	Diameter	Circumference ÷ Diameter

What conclusion is suggested by the results in the last column?

Discovering the relationship between circumference and diameter
Gathering data
Placing results in tabular form

Calculator Math Level E © 1995 Fearon Teacher Aids

Chess Master

Just a few grains of rice.

This is a famous tale about the game of chess.

The game's inventor presented it to his king and queen who were totally thrilled by the game. As a reward, they offered him anything he wanted, expecting he would ask for a bag of diamonds or bars of gold. Instead, the seemingly insignificant reward the inventor asked for was:

"1 grain of rice for the first square on the chess board, 2 for the second, 4 for the third, 8 for the fourth, and so on."

The king and queen granted his request immediately. They thought all the man wanted was a few bags of rice. Boy, were they wrong!

Complete the table, showing the rice required for the FIRST TWO ROWS on the chess board.

SQUARE	CALCULATION	GRAINS OF RICE
1	1	1
2	1×2	2
3	2×2	4
4	2×2×2	8
5	2×2×2×2	16
6	2×2×2×2×2	32
7	2×2×2×2×2×2	64
8	2×2×2×2×2×2×2	128
9	2×2×2×2×2×2×2×2	256
10	etc.	
11		
12		
13		
14		
15		
16		

Exponents

Calculator Math Level E © 1995 Fearon Teacher Aids

Best Buys

Who's the smartest shopper?

Circle the "best buys" for each item.

ITEM	BRAND A		BRAND B	
	Size	Cost	Size	Cost
Chips	50 g	20¢	40 g	19¢
Onions	1 kg	39¢	1.5 kg	50¢
Pickles	750 mL	2 for $1.49	800 mL	3 for $2.09
Hamburger	800 g	$1.47	900 g	$1.60
Cheese	0.5 kg pack	2 packs for $1.49	0.75 kg pack	$1.07
Apples	10	98¢ a dozen	10	2 for 19¢
Jelly	50 mL	3 for 89¢	25 mL	7 for $1.00
Pop	300 mL	6 for $1.49	750 mL	33¢ each
Bread	500 g	3 for $1.45	750 g	2 for $1.45
Soap	100 g	2 for 63¢	150 g	3 for 99¢

Working with ratio
Developing consumer awareness
Using the calculator judiciously

One of Everything

Place your order.

Mr. Ownamint was a rich, but impatient man. He wanted to buy a few items from a catalogue, but hated bothering with order forms. So, he phoned the company, gave them his credit card number and said, "Send me one of everything."

1. To estimate the cost of such an order, select a catalogue and find the total cost of all the items on an entire page. Your classmates will do the same.

2. Use all the results to calculate the average total cost per page.

3. Use that average to estimate the total cost of Mr. Ownamint's order.

4. Repeat the experiment (steps 1-3), using new pages at random. What is the relative difference between the estimates?

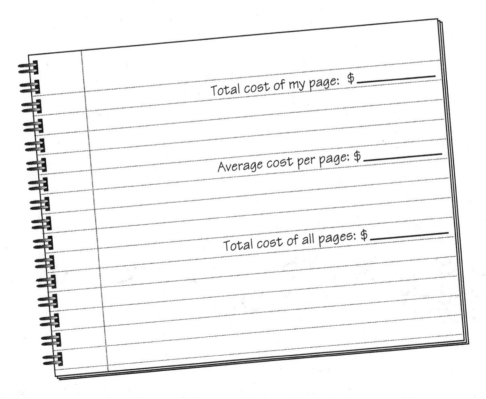

Total cost of my page: $ _____

Average cost per page: $ _____

Total cost of all pages: $ _____

Gathering data
Finding averages
Estimation

Calculator Math Level E © 1995 Fearon Teacher Aids

Batter Up!

Who's the best batter?

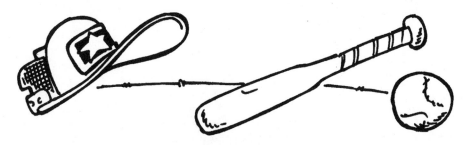

Complete the table.
(Calculations for the first line are shown below.)

Name	Hits	Times at Bat	Batting Average	
Jones	84	304	0.276	
Berstein	95	310	.306	
Duncan	83	340	.244	
Washington	96	295	.325	
Kew	26	141	.184	
Park	37	162	.228	
Brown	121	351	.345	
Kolinski	134	400	.335	
Suavé	85	304	.279	
Totals	761	2,607	2.522	**Team Average**

Jones' Batting Average	=	Hits ÷ Times at Bat
	=	84 ÷ 304
	=	0.2763157
	=	0.276

1. Which player would be the best choice for your team? Explain.

   Brown, because he/she has the highest average.

2. Can the team average be found in two ways? Explain.

   You can add all the averages, or add all the hits and divide by all the Times at bat.

If the Shoe Fits

Gather and organize data.

Buy running shoes for your family.

Men's
$74.99

Women's
$69.99

Children's
$47.50

Total Cost: _____

Count the shoelace eyelets in your shoes.
Choose five friends and count their shoelace eyelets.
(Write "0" if someone wears shoes without eyelets.)

Complete the table.

Name	Number of Eyelets

a. Find the average number of eyelets per person in the group.

b. Use this average to get an estimate for the number of shoe eyelets in your class.

c. Use the average to estimate the number of shoe eyelets in your state, assuming everyone owns four pairs of shoes.

d. What are some of the assumptions you made to solve these problems?

Gathering data
Finding averages and ratios

Calculator Math Level E © 1995 Fearon Teacher Aids

Faster Than a Speeding Snail

Process data with your calculator.

Examine the table of top running speeds of humans and various animals.

ANIMAL	SPEED (km/h)	ANIMAL	SPEED (km/h)
Pig	17.5	Greyhound	63
Quarter Horse	76.5	Gray Fox	67.5
Rabbit	56	Grizzly Bear	48
Zebra	64	Human	45
Lion	80	Chicken	14.5
Garden Snail	0.05	Tortoise	0.27
Cheetah	112	Sloth	0.24

1. Arrange the animals in order of speed.

2. Find the ratios, comparing the top speed of the animals with that of humans.

3. Write your results in the graph (page 62).

Calculating ratios
Constructing graphs
Using constants

Ratio of Top Running Speed of Animals to Top Running Speed of Humans

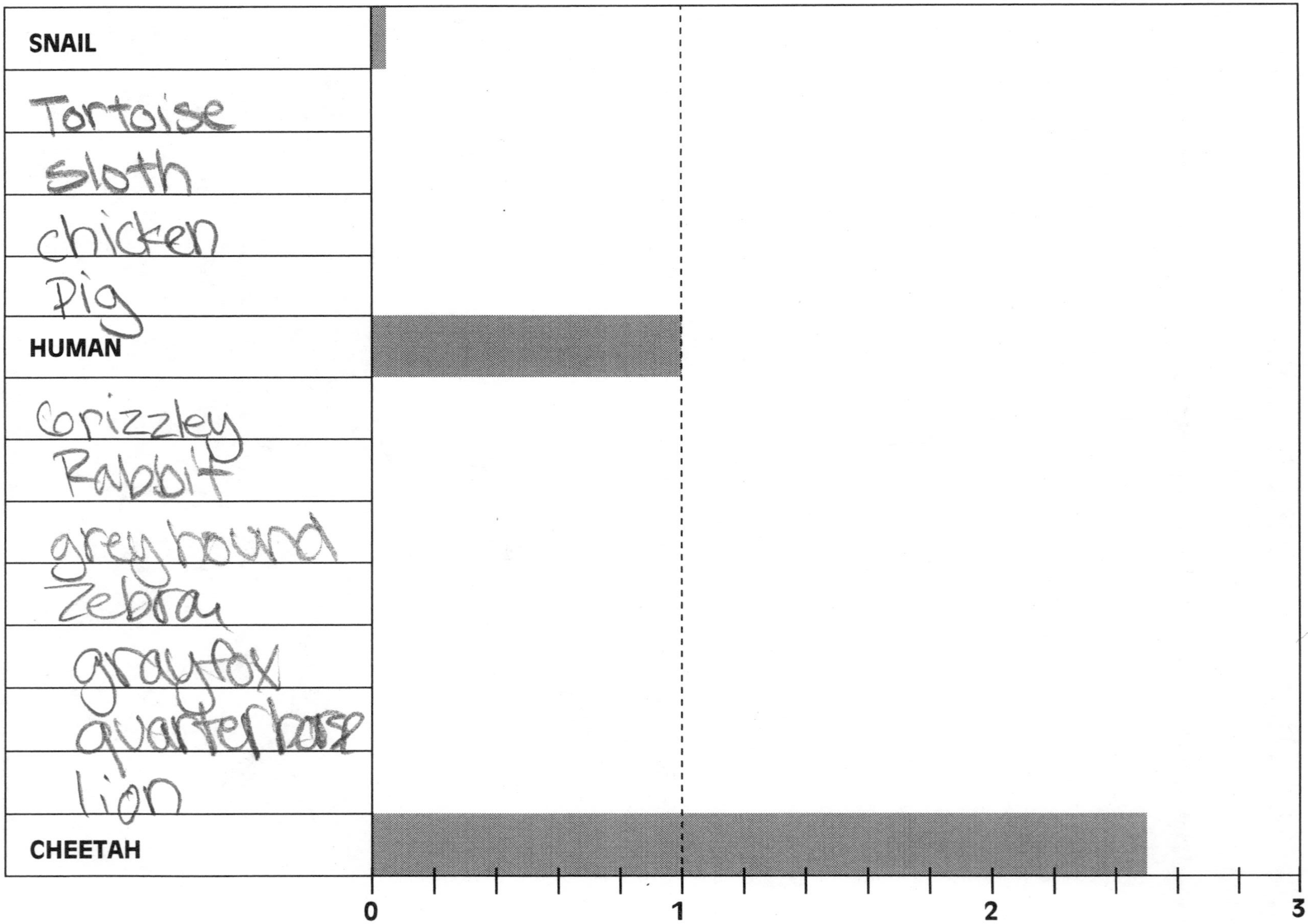

SNAIL

Tortoise

Sloth

Chicken

Pig

HUMAN

Grizzley

Rabbit

greyhound

Zebra

grayfox

quarterhorse

lion

CHEETAH

Calculator Math Level E © 1995 Fearon Teacher Aids

Soda Pop Challenge

More data to collect and refine.

Ask five friends how many bottles or cans (300 mL) of soda pop they drank each day during the last week.

Complete the table and calculate the totals, including yourself.

Name	Day 1	Day 2	Day 3	Day 4	Day 5	Day 6	Day 7	Total
Total								

1. Calculate the average amount of soda pop you and your friends drank per day.

_____

_____

2. At today's prices, how much would a year's supply of soda pop cost for you and your friends?

_____

_____

Gathering data
Finding averages and ratios
Developing consumer awareness
Reading and constructing tables

Thinking Through the Problem

Plan your strategy.

1. How could you get the number "5" in your calculator display using only the
   [+] , [−] , [×] , [÷] , and [2] keys?

   $(2 \times 2 \times 2) + 2 \div 2$

2. Light travels at a speed of 297,650 km/second.
   How far is that in one hour?

   1071540000

3. If today was your 12th birthday, how many days
   old would you be?

   4380

4. How would you find 432 × 725 on your calculator if
   neither the [3] nor the [4] keys were working?

   $(422 + 10) \times 725 = 313200$

5. During figure skating competition, Peggy obtained these scores: 9.5, 8.7, 8,4, and 8.8.
   What was her average score?   8.85

6. A complicated computer job is estimated to take a million seconds. How long is that
   (in minutes/hours/days/weeks)?

   min 16666.666

   hrs. 277.7776

   weeks 11.5

7. The price tag for a soda pop sale reads
   "3/$1.00." How much would it cost you to
   buy five cans? $1.66

8. How old will you be (in years) when you
   are 5000 days old?

   13.69863

9. The annual membership fee at a golf club
   went up from $400 to $500. The cost per
   game went down from $12 to $8. After how
   many games are the new rates better?

   After 25 games

Calculator Math Level E © 1995 Fearon Teacher Aids

Name _____

A Day in Your Life

How do you spend your time?

Estimate how many hours per **Tuesday** you spend at the following activities. Write your estimates in the first column. Then, ask five of your classmates to complete the next five columns. Complete the table.

Activity	Number of Hours							
	You	Friend A	Friend B	Friend C	Friend D	Friend E	Total	Average
Sleeping	9							
Eating	$\frac{1}{4}$							
Playing	2							
Helping	0							
Watching Television	6							
Reading	0							
Attending School	6							
Total	23⅓							

Using the average results from the table above, complete this chart.

Activity	Number of Minutes	Percentage of the Time
Sleeping	540	738.38
Eating	15	209.25%
Playing	120	167%
Helping	0	0
Watching Television	360	
Reading	0	0
Attending School	360	
Total	1395	

Gathering data
Finding averages and percentages
Reading and constructing tables

65

Money Matters

How good are you with money?

1. Up in Smoke

Find out the cost of a pack of cigarettes. What would it cost to buy one pack daily for:

1 year? _____   40 years? _____

Check with a person who smokes to find out how many packs per day he or she smokes. Compute his or her smoking cost per year.

2. Heavy Expenses

Find the mass of each item.

penny: _____ g

nickel: _____ g

dime: _____ g

quarter: _____ g

dollar bill: _____ g

Calculate the mass of $100 in:

pennies: _____

nickels: _____

dimes: _____

quarters: _____

dollar bills: _____

3. Discount Baby-sitting

Bill's Baby Business is announcing a special for November. Baby-sitting rates are $1.00 per hour for the first child, half of that for the second child, half of the cost of the second child for the third child, and so on.

a. Find Bill's rate per hour for 2 children. _____

b. For 3 children. _____

c. For 6 children. _____

d. What is his maximum rate per hour? _____

Collecting data
Finding the mass of an object
Conceptualizing limits
Finding rates

Calculator Math Level E © 1995 Fearon Teacher Aids

Going in Circles II
Solve problems working with pi.

1. The world record for Ferris wheel riding is 21 days, 3 hours, and 58 minutes. During that time, the rider traveled 1158.728 km (in circles) in 11,800 revolutions.

    a. What was the diameter of the wheel? _31.26_

    b. How long did the wheel take to travel one revolution? _2min_

    c. How long did the rider take to travel one km? _26min_

    d. What was the speed of the wheel in revolutions per minute? _39 rv_

    e. What was the speed of the rider in kilometers per hour? _2.26 Kmh_

2. You need a new tire for your car. The tire you decide to buy is steel-belted for safety and treadwear-rated at 40,000 km.

        Cost: $67.50   **Diameter:** 83 cm

        Cost per kilometer = _.0016875_

    Number of revolutions required to go 40,000 km = _15,340,234_

Working with pi
Working with ratios
Finding rates of speed

Name _____

Burger Business

Work with larger facts.

A certain hamburger chain claims to have sold 20,000,000,000 hamburgers.
The average hamburger has 100 g of meat, 2.5 mL of ketchup, and 0.3 g of salt.

1. If a cow yields 150 kg of beef, how many cows were needed for these hamburgers?

   13,333,333

2. How many tanker trucks, each holding 6 m³, would be needed to deliver the ketchup?

   8,335

3. How many tons of salt were used?

   6,000 tons

For Experts

Create your own problem about the pickles or onions found in some of the hamburgers.
Give this problem to a classmate to solve.

Calculator Math Level E © 1995 Fearon Teacher Aids

Working with large numbers
Working with ratios

Hummingbird Trivia

Discover some incredible numbers.

Some Facts About Hummingbirds

▼ The giant hummingbird grows up to 21 cm long and weighs 20 g. The bee hummingbird is 6.25 cm long and weighs 2 g.

▼ A hummingbird's tongue licks nectar at a rate of 13 licks per second. It can lick 3-8 g of nectar from a feeder at one time.

▼ Hummingbirds eat more than half their body weight in food and drink eight times their weight in water each day.

▼ Hummingbirds need 6660 to 12,400 calories per day. They use 35 calories per minute to hover. (Humans need about 2500 kilo calories per day, i.e., 2,500,000 "hummingbird" calories.)

▼ Hummingbird hearts beat from 480 to 1260 times per minute. They breathe about 250 times per minute. (Humans breathe about 16 times per minute.)

▼ Ruby-throated hummingbirds fly at up to 48 km per hour (they can dive at 128 km/h). Their wings beat an average of 52 times per second.

▼ Ruby-throated hummingbirds migrate up to 3200 km (Nova Scotia to Panama), including an 800 km non-stop trip over open ocean. A ruby-throat can fly for up to 26 hours before landing.

▼ Hummingbird eggs are less than 1.25 cm long and weigh less than 5 g.

Problems

1. How many times will a ruby-throated hummingbird's heart beat in an hour? 28800-75600/h

2. How many heartbeats will the ruby-throated hummingbird experience during its non-stop ocean crossing? How many breaths? How many wing beats? 1352 wb, 748800 hb, 390000 b

3. A full grown ostrich weighs about 140 kg. How many bee hummingbirds would it take to weigh the same? 280 bee hummingbird

Using these hummingbird facts, create some problems of your own to exchange with a classmate. See if you can solve them.

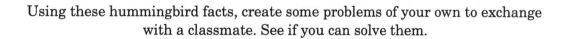

Integration with science
Reading carefully for information
Problem solving

69

For Calculating Experts

Now that you're an expert . . .

1. Find 888 × 88 on your calculator without using the [8] key.

2. Use your calculator to find the remainders for these division problems.

    a. 89 ÷ 8   11.125

    b. 75 ÷ 6   12.5

    c. 29 ÷ 3   9.666

    d. 539 ÷ 29   18.586206

    e. 7931 ÷ 267   29.704119

3. Use each of the digits [1] [2] [3] [4] [5] [6] [7] [8] once to make two 4-digit numbers with the largest possible product.   8543 × 761 =

4. Use each of the digits [1] [2] [3] [4] [5] [6] [7] [8] once to make two 4-digit numbers with the smallest possible product.   2×1×8×6×7×3×4×5

5. Use each of the digits [2] [3] [4] [5] [6] [7] once to make two numbers with the largest possible product. (You can make this problem easier by changing it to one with an even number of digits.)   634 × 752

6. Use each of the digits [2] [3] [4] [5] [6] [7] once to make two numbers with the smallest possible product.   234 × 567

7. Use each of the digits [1] [2] [3] [4] [5] [6] [7] [8] [9] once to make three 3-digit numbers with the largest possible product.   987 × 654 × 321

8. Use each of the digits [1] [2] [3] [4] [5] [6] [7] [8] [9] once to make three 3-digit numbers with the smallest possible product.
     123 × 456

Advanced place value applications
Problem solving

Calculator Math Level E © 1995 Fearon Teacher Aids

Problem Solving

Name _____

Friends in Numbers
Working with number patterns.

1. Three people give each other birthday presents. How many presents are there all together? What if there had been four people? Fill in the chart.

Number of People	Number of Presents
2	2
3	6
4	12
5	20
6	30
8	42
10	80
18	288

Can you find a formula that gives the number of presents for any group of people?

2. Three people are introduced to each other and shake hands. How many handshakes are there all together? What if there had been four people? Complete the chart to show the number of handshakes for other groups.

Number of People	Number of Shakes
2	1
3	3
4	6
5	10
6	15
8	28
10	45
18	158

Can you find a formula that gives the number of handshakes for any group of people?

Calculator Math Level E © 1995 Fearon Teacher Aids

Answer Key

This section provides solutions for all activity sheets having exact answers. In estimation exercises, student approximations are more important than exact answers. The answers provided here should then be viewed only as examples. Some activity sheets are not included in this section. These are noted in sequence for easy reference.

The Cost of Money I

Simple interest—how much you pay.

Work through the following example.

Example

Deposit or Loan (Principal): $100
Interest Rate: 8%
Interest after 1 year = *$8*
Total owing after 1 year = *$108*

Solution

8% of $100 = 0.08 × $100 = $8
Interest = $8
Total owing = $100 (principal) + $8 (interest)
= $108

Look at the example. Your calculator can perform this type of operation.

Punch in [1][0][0][+][8][%]. The display shows "8." This is the interest. Push [=].
The display shows "108." This is the total (principal + interest). Try the example again.

It is possible to find the total (principal + interest) in one step without using the [%] key.
For the example, the steps would be: [1][0][0][×][1][.][0][8][=]
100% (principal) + 8% (interest)

The display would read "108."
By subtracting the principal (100), you can find the interest (108 − 100 = 8).

1. Principal: $250
   Interest Rate: 9%
   Interest: *$22.50*
   Total owing (after 1 year): *$272.50*

2. Find the value after 1 year of:
   $87.49 invested at 9%: *$95.36*
   $2645 invested at 12%: *$2962.40*

3.

Principal	Rate	Interest	Total After 1 Year
$460.00	4%	*$18.40*	*$478.40*
$625.49	9%	*$56.29*	*$681.78*
$4000.00	11%	*$440.00*	*$4440.00*
$256.33	7%	*$17.94*	*$274.27*
$5847.00	9.5%	*$555.47*	*$6402.47*

Introducing the % key
Using the calculator effectively
Developing consumer awareness

The Cost of Money II

Calculate more simple interest.

Money is often borrowed or deposited for longer periods of time. In these cases, simple interest is computed on the original amount (the principal) every year.

Example

Principal: $300
Interest Rate: 6%
Loan Period: 4 years
Interest per year: *$18.00*
Interest for 4 years: *$72.00*
Interest + principal: *$372.00*

Solution

Interest for 1 year = $300 × 0.06
= $18
Interest for 4 years = $18 × 4
= $72
Total = $300 + $72
= $372

Fast Method

Push: [3][0][0][+][6][%][=][=][=][=]
4 years

1. Interest Rate: 14%
   Period: 2 years
   Total Payable: *$1111.03*

   $867.99

2. Interest Rate: 7%
   Period: 4 years
   Total after 4 years: *$3160.32*

   $2469.00 (savings account)

3.

Principal	Rate	Period	Interest	Total Payable
$420.25	12%	3 years	*$151.29*	*$571.54*
$1200.72	9.5%	5 years	*$570.34*	*$1771.06*
$1935.72	14%	15 years	*$4065.01*	*$6000.73*
$318.75	10%	12 years	*$382.50*	*$701.25*
$100.00	18%	50 years	*$900.00*	*$1000.00*

Introducing the % key
Using the calculator effectively
Developing consumer awareness

The State's Little Bit Extra

Figure sales tax.

Exercise 1

Assuming a sales tax of 7%, find the total cost for articles priced as follows:

Cost	Cost + Sales Tax
$7.00	$7.49
$12.00	12.84
$8.00	8.56
$2.00	2.14
$4.70	5.03
Total Bill	36.06

Find the total cost without sales tax first. Then calculate the tax for that total amount.
Is the total bill any different? **NO**

This is an illustration of the distributive property.

Explain. $1.07 \times 33.70 = (1.07 \times 7) + (1.07 \times 12) + (1.07 \times 8) + (1.07 \times 2) + (1.07 \times 4.70)$

Exercise 2

Assuming a sales tax of 6%, find the total cost for articles priced as follows:

Cost	Cost + Sales Tax
$5.00	$5.30
$4.80	5.09
$2.44	2.59
$7.30	7.74
$5.60	5.94
Total Bill	26.66

Use your calculator to find the total cost and then add the sales tax.
Is there a difference? Explain.

Yes. $26.65 (a difference of $.01)

Which method of calculating the total bill is fairer? Why?

The second method. In the first, it is possible that accumulated rounding errors will cause a cost difference.

Using the % key
Understanding taxation

Money, Money in the Bank I

Understanding compound interest.

Joan's grandfather gave her $100 to open a savings account.
At the end of each year, the bank pays 6% interest and adds it to the account.
Complete the table to show how Joan's account increases.

Principal: $100   Interest Rate: 6%   Term: 5 years (compound interest)

	Principal $		Interest $		Total $
Year 1	100	+	$100 \times 0.06 = 6$	=	$100 + 6 = 106$
Year 2	106	+	6.36	=	112.36
Year 3	112.36	+	6.74	=	119.10
Year 4	119.10	+	7.15	=	126.25
Year 5	126.25	+	7.58	=	133.83

Interest which is added to the account each year to form the principal for the following year is called *compound interest.* What is the difference between simple interest and compound interest?

You pay interest on last year's interest if it's compounded

Which is more? **Compound** Why? **interest on interest**

Complete the table below.

Principal: $100   Rate: 7%   Term: 6 years

	Principal $	Principal + Interest (Total) $
Year 1	100	107
Year 2	107	114.49
Year 3	114.49	122.50
Year 4	122.50	131.08
Year 5	131.08	140.25
Year 6	140.25	150.07

Calculator key sequence:
1 . 0 7 × 1 0 0 = 107
or 1 0 0 + 7 %

Understanding compound interest
Using the calculator effectively

Money, Money in the Bank II

How compound interest adds up.

1. Complete the table.

Principal: $100   Rate of Interest: 8%   Loan Period: 5 years

Years	Principal + Interest Method A `1 0 0 + 8 % =`	Principal + Interest Method B `1 0 0 × 1 . 0 8 =`
1	108.00	108.00
2	116.00	116.64
3	124.00	125.97
4	132.00	136.05
5	140.00	146.93

Discuss the differences between the two methods.

A. *Simple interest*

B. *Compound interest*

2. Use the methods shown above to complete the table.

Principal	Rate	Period	Total (Simple Interest)	Total (compound interest)
$400	7%	2 years	456.00	457.96
$960	12%	3 years	1305.60	1348.73
$1435	15%	5 years	2511.25	2886.30
$2869	18%	7 years	6483.94	9139.12
$5000	10%	10 years	10,000.00	12,968.71

3. The family Mark baby-sat for was so pleased with his work that they paid him a 10% increase over the previous year's rate at each of his birthdays. Mark decided to make a career out of baby-sitting for this family. He sat for nieces and nephews, for the children's children, and finally for great-grandchildren. He started at age 12 for $1.00 per hour. At age 85, he was still sitting for the same family. What was his hourly rate by this time? $10,571.15

Using the % key
Understanding compound interest

23

For activity sheet "Bermuda Triangles" on page 24, triangles A, D, E, G, H, and I are the "Bermuda" triangles.

Calculator Math Level E © 1995 Fearon Teacher Aids

Name _____

All-Star Estimating
Consider the decimals first.

Estimate each product to at least two significant digits.
Check your estimates with your calculator.

Exact answers given. Estimates may vary.

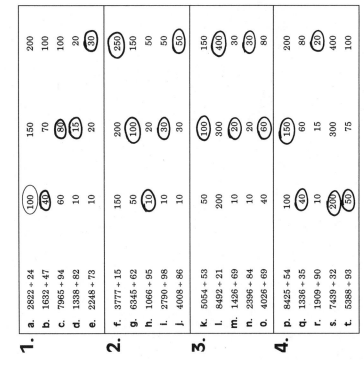

Rounding with decimals
Estimating in multiplication

Name _____

Divide and Figure
Rounding will help you.

Circle the answer which is the best estimate for each quotient.
Check your estimates with the calculator. The first one is done for you.

1.	a. 2822 ÷ 24	(100)	150	200
	b. 1632 ÷ 47	(40)	70	100
	c. 7965 ÷ 94	60	(80)	100
	d. 1338 ÷ 82	10	(15)	20
	e. 2248 ÷ 73	10	20	(30)
2.	f. 3777 ÷ 15	150	200	(250)
	g. 6345 ÷ 62	50	(100)	150
	h. 1066 ÷ 95	(10)	20	50
	i. 2790 ÷ 98	10	(30)	50
	j. 4008 ÷ 86	10	30	(50)
3.	k. 5054 ÷ 53	50	(100)	150
	l. 8492 ÷ 21	200	300	(400)
	m. 1426 ÷ 69	10	(20)	30
	n. 2396 ÷ 84	10	20	(30)
	o. 4026 ÷ 69	40	(60)	80
4.	p. 8425 ÷ 54	100	(150)	200
	q. 1336 ÷ 35	(40)	60	80
	r. 1909 ÷ 90	10	15	(20)
	s. 7439 ÷ 32	(200)	300	400
	t. 5388 ÷ 93	(50)	75	100

Estimating in division
Rounding in division

For the "Games" section on pages 27-34, answers will vary.

Name _____

A Decimal by Another Name

Convert decimals to fractions.

Fractions

1. If you divide 312 by 4 and multiply your answer by 4, what do you think your answer will be? __**312**__

   Try it on your calculator.

2. If you divide any counting number by 4 and multiply your answer by 4, what do you think your answer will be? __**The same number**__

   Try it on your calculator. Write down five examples. **Answers will vary.**

   a. _____ b. _____ c. _____ d. _____ e. _____

3. A number is divided by 4. The answer is 1.25. What was the original number? __**5**__

4. A number is divided by 8. The result is 0.375. What was the original number? __**3**__

5. 0.375 equals what fraction? __**3/8**__

6. A number is divided by 25. The result is 0.92. What was the number divided by 25? __**23**__

7. The decimal fraction $0.92 = \frac{23}{25}$

8. Change the following decimal fractions to fractions with the required numerators.

$0.3 = \frac{3}{10}$ $0.4 = \frac{2}{5}$ $0.75 = \frac{3}{4}$ $0.3125 = \frac{5}{16}$ $0.625 = \frac{5}{8}$

$0.095 = \frac{19}{200}$ $0.6 = \frac{9}{15}$ $0.064 = \frac{8}{125}$ $0.2125 = \frac{17}{80}$ $0.75 = \frac{24}{32}$

How can you show that $\frac{3}{4} = \frac{24}{32}$?

$\frac{3}{4} = 0.75, \frac{24}{32} = 0.75, \text{ therefore, } \frac{3}{4} = \frac{24}{32}$

(Think: $\frac{3}{4} = 0.75 = \frac{?}{32}$)

Converting decimals to fractions
Working with equivalent fractions

35

Calculator Math Level E © 1995 Fearon Teacher Aids

Name _____

It's All Equal
Converting fractions made easy.

Use your calculator to convert $\frac{3}{5}$ to another fraction with a denominator of 25.

The answer should be: $\frac{3}{5} = \frac{15}{25}$.

Similarly, change the following fractions to equivalent forms.

- $\frac{1}{5} = \frac{4}{20}$
- $\frac{3}{8} = \frac{12}{32}$
- $\frac{2}{5} = \frac{16}{40}$
- $\frac{5}{8} = \frac{35}{56}$
- $\frac{9}{12} = \frac{150}{200}$
- $\frac{4}{20} = \frac{18}{90}$
- $\frac{70}{280} = \frac{18}{72}$
- $\frac{20}{32} = \frac{15}{24}$
- $\frac{18}{84} = \frac{15}{20}$
- $\frac{36}{48} = \frac{48}{64}$

Name _____

Calculating Fractions I
How does a calculator handle fractions?

Most calculators are not capable of showing common fractions on their displays. Therefore, common fractions are usually changed to decimals.

Exercise A
Change these to decimal fractions.

$\frac{1}{2} =$ **0.5**

$\frac{5}{8} =$ **0.625**

$\frac{3}{4} =$ **0.75**

How would you compute the decimal fraction for $\frac{27}{45}$? **27 ÷ 45**

Exercise B
Add these fractions, showing all your work. Change your answer to a decimal fraction.

$\frac{2}{5} + \frac{3}{4} =$

Your work should look like:

$\frac{2}{5} + \frac{3}{4} = \frac{2 \times 4}{5 \times 4} + \frac{3 \times 5}{4 \times 5}$
$= \frac{8}{20} + \frac{15}{20}$
$= \frac{23}{20}$
$= 1\frac{3}{20}$
$= 1\frac{15}{100}$
$= 1.15$

It's easier to change each fraction to a decimal first, and then add.
For example:

$\frac{2}{5} + \frac{3}{4} = 0.4 + 0.75 = 1.15$

Exercise C
Add these fractions, showing all your work.

1. $\frac{3}{4} + \frac{7}{8} =$

2. $\frac{1}{2} + \frac{7}{16} =$

Your work should look like:

1. $\frac{3}{4} + \frac{7}{8} = 0.75 + 0.875 = 1.625$
2. $\frac{1}{2} + \frac{7}{16} = 0.5 + 0.4375 = 0.9375$

Exercise D
Add these fractions, showing all your work.

1. $\frac{9}{25} + \frac{36}{64} =$ **0.36 + 0.5625 = 0.9225**

2. $\frac{15}{24} + \frac{35}{40} =$ **0.625 + 0.875 = 1.5**

Adding and subtracting common fractions
Using the calculator effectively
Working with the distributive property
Working with calculator algorithms

37

Name _____

Calculating Fractions II

More on how the calculator handles fractions.

Exercise A

Add $\frac{1}{2} + \frac{7}{16}$

You should have punched in [1] [÷] [2] [×] [1] [6] [+] [7] [÷] [1] [6]

Correct answer: 0.9375

Add these fractions, using your calculator.

1. $\frac{5}{8} + \frac{1}{4} =$ **0.875**
2. $\frac{17}{20} + \frac{4}{5} =$ **1.65**
3. $\frac{6}{10} + \frac{19}{40} =$ **1.075**
4. $\frac{5}{16} + \frac{1}{2} =$ **0.8125**

Exercise B

Example: $\frac{3}{4} - \frac{1}{2} =$ [3] [÷] [4] [×] [2] [−] [1] [÷] [2] = 0.25

Subtract these fractions, using your calculator.

1. $\frac{5}{8} - \frac{3}{10} =$ **0.325**
2. $\frac{15}{16} - \frac{3}{4} =$ **0.1875**
3. $\frac{7}{8} - \frac{13}{40} =$ **0.55**
4. $\frac{9}{16} - \frac{1}{2} =$ **0.0625**

Exercise C

Examples:

I. $\frac{3}{4} + \frac{1}{2} + 6$ = [3] [÷] [4] [×] [2] [+] [1] [÷] [2] [+] [6] = 7.25

II. $\frac{3}{4} + \frac{1}{2} + 8$ = [3] [÷] [4] [×] [2] [+] [1] [÷] [2] [×] [8] [+] [8] = 1.875

1. $\frac{3}{4} + \frac{7}{16} + \frac{11}{40} =$ **1.4625**
2. $\frac{3}{10} + \frac{7}{8} + \frac{5}{16} =$ **1.2875**
3. $\frac{3}{8} + 5 - \frac{1}{2} =$ **0.275**
4. $6 - \frac{1}{16} - \frac{3}{20} =$ **0.5375**

Adding and subtracting common fractions
Using the calculator effectively
Working with the distributive property
Working with calculator algorithms

Name _____

Fast Fractions

How you can help your calculator.

Exercise A

1. $\frac{3}{7} \times 4 =$ **1.7142857**
2. $\frac{2}{5} \times 12 =$ **4.8**
3. $5 \times \frac{2}{9} =$ **1.11111**
4. $8 \times \frac{4}{3} =$ **10.666666**

Multiply $\frac{7}{16} \times \frac{5}{8}$ on your calculator. Your answer should be 0.4375.
What is one way to perform this operation?

[7] [×] [5] [÷] [1O] [÷] [8]

Exercise B

1. $\frac{5}{6} \times \frac{9}{10} =$ **0.75**
2. $\frac{3}{4} \times \frac{5}{8} =$ **0.46875**
3. $\frac{3}{8} \times \frac{7}{5} =$ **0.525**
4. $\frac{4}{14} \times \frac{7}{4} =$ **0.5**
5. $\frac{13}{29} \times \frac{5}{26} =$ **0.0862068**

Exercise C

1. $\frac{5}{8} \times \frac{4}{6} \times \frac{9}{10} =$ **0.375**
2. $\frac{7}{16} \times \frac{2}{5} \times \frac{5}{12} =$ **0.0729166**
3. $\frac{3}{8} \times \frac{5}{8} \times \frac{33}{8} =$ **2.1484375**
4. $\frac{4}{15} \times \frac{5}{26} \times \frac{100}{3} =$ **1.709401**

Using the calculator effectively
Multiplying fractions
Working with calculator algorithms

Pattern Discovery

Name _____

Discover your own pattern.

Consider the array below.

```
 1  ②  3   4   5   6   7   8   9  10
⑪  22  23  24  25  26  27  28  29  30
21  32  33  34  35  36  37  38  39  40
31  ㊴  43  ㉞  ㉟  46  47  48  49  ㊿
㊶  ㊷  53  ㊹  ㊺  56  57  58  59  ㊳
51  62  63  64  65  66  ㊻  68  69  ㊽
61  72  73  74  ㊄  76  ㊲  78  79  80
71  82  83  84  85  86  87  88  89  90
81  92  93  94  95  96  97  98  99 100
91
```

1. Compare the pair 34, 45 with the pair 44, 35.

a. **Add:**   34 + 45 = __79__
         44 + 35 = __79__

What do you notice about the answers?
__They're the same__

Is that true for any two such pairs?
__yes__

b. **Subtract:** 45 – 34 = __11__
            44 – 35 = __9__

How do the answers differ?
__by 2__

Is that true for any two such pairs?
__yes__

c. **Multiply:** 34 × 45 = __1530__
            35 × 44 = __1540__

How do the answers differ?
__by 10__

Is that true for any two such pairs?
__yes__

2. Describe some of the patterns you found.
Do they hold true if the array is extended
to include negative numbers?
__See hints drawn on array.__
_____

3. What happens to your pattern if the
array is changed as follows?

1	2	3	4	5	6
7	8	9	10	11	12
13	14	15	16	17	18
19	20	21	22	23	24

__+, the same__
__–, always 7, 5 (differ by 2)__
__×, differ by 6__

Be a Number Detective I

Name _____

Can you predict the patterns?

1. **Use your calculator:**

1 ÷ 3 = __0.3333333__

Predict:

1000 ÷ __3333__ = __0.3003000__ _(0.3000300)_

10,000 ÷ __33,333__ = __0.3003003__ _(0.3000030)_

100,000 ÷ __333,333__ = __0.3003003__ _(0.3000003)_

Check your guesses.

2. **Use your calculator:**

1 ÷ 7 = __0.1428571__

2 ÷ 7 = __0.2857142__

3 ÷ 7 = __0.4285714__

Predict:

4 ÷ 7 = __0.5714285__

__5__ ÷ 7 = __0.7142857__

__6__ ÷ __7__ = __0.8571428__

Hint: Notice the order of the digits.

3. **Use your calculator:**

1 × 9 = __9__

11 × 99 = __1089__

111 × 999 = __110,889__

1111 × 9999 = __11,108,889__

Predict:

11,111 × 99,999 = __1,111,088,889__

111,111 × 999,999 = __111,110,888,889__

Name _____

Be a Number Detective II

Discover more patterns.

Complete the pattern.

$$1 = 1 = 1^2$$
$$1 + 3 = 4 = 2^2$$
$$1 + 3 + 5 = 9 = 3^2$$
$$1 + 3 + 5 + 7 = 16 = 4^2$$
$$1 + 3 + 5 + 7 + 9 = 25 = 5^2$$
$$1 + 3 + 5 + 7 + 9 + 11 = 36 = 6^2$$
$$1 + 3 + 5 + 7 + 9 + 11 + 13 = 49 = 7^2$$

Guess: $1 + 3 + 5 \ldots + 19 = 100 = 10^2$

1. To understand what is happening, count the number of dots in each section of the square.

(rows labeled: 1, 3, 5, 7, 9, 11)

This figure is a square containing 6 × 6 dots.
Therefore, $1 + 3 + 5 + 7 + 9 + 11 = 6^2$.

2. Complete the diagram below to illustrate the sum:
$$1 + 3 + 5 + 7 + 9 + 11 + 13 + 15$$

(rows labeled: 1, 3, 5, 7, 9, 11, 13, 15)

Write the corresponding number sentence.

$$1 + 3 + 5 + 7 + 9 + 11 + 13 + 15 = 64 = 8^2$$

Use your calculator to check whether $1 + 3 + 5 + 7 + \ldots + 31$ is a perfect square.

Yes $256 = 16^2$

Detecting and completing patterns
Explaining patterns
Squaring and square roots

42

Name _____

Be a Square Detective

Showing squares with dot patterns.

Complete the pattern.

$$1 = 1 = 1^2$$
$$1 + 2 + 1 = 4 = 2^2$$
$$1 + 2 + 3 + 2 + 1 = 9 = 3^2$$
$$1 + 2 + 3 + 4 + 3 + 2 + 1 = 16 = 4^2$$
$$1 + 2 + 3 + 4 + 5 + 4 + 3 + 2 + 1 = 25 = 5^2$$
$$1 + 2 + 3 + 4 + 5 + 6 + 5 + 4 + 3 + 2 + 1 = 36 = 6^2$$

Now guess:

$$1 + 2 + 3 + 4 + 5 + 6 + 7 + 8 + 9 + 10 + 9 + 8 + 7 + 6 + 5 + 4 + 3 + 2 + 1 = 100 = 10^2$$

Use this dot pattern to explain what is happening.

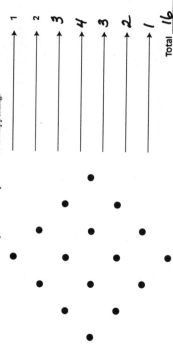

(arrows labeled: 1, 2, 3, 4, 3, 2, 1   Total 16)

The figure is a square containing $\underline{4} \times \underline{4} = (\underline{4})^2$ dots.
Therefore, $1 + 2 + 3 + 4 + 3 + 2 + 1 = (\underline{4})^2$.

Draw a similar dot diagram on the back of this sheet to explain why
$$1 + 2 + 3 + 4 + 5 + 4 + 3 + 2 + 1 = 5^2.$$

Detecting and explaining patterns
Squaring and square roots

43

Calculator Math Level E © 1995 Fearon Teacher Aids

Left worksheet

Name _____

The Three-Angle Detective

Discover dot patterns for triangles.

1	=	1
1 + 2	=	3
1 + 2 + 3	=	6
1 + 2 + 3 + 4	=	10
1 + 2 + 3 + 4 + 5	=	15
1 + 2 + 3 + 4 + 5 + 6	=	21
1 + 2 + 3 + 4 + 5 + 6 + 7	=	28

4	=	2^2
9	=	3^2
16	=	4^2
25	=	5^2
36	=	6^2
49	=	7^2

The numbers 1, 3, 6, 10, and so on, are called *triangular numbers*. Look at the dot patterns to see why.

What happens when one triangular number is added to the next? Explain, using the dot pattern below. *A square is formed.*

The two triangular arrays combine to form a square array.

The bottom row of the larger triangular array forms a diagonal of the square.

Detecting and completing patterns
Explaining patterns
Squaring and square roots

Right worksheet

Name _____

Pattern Power

Can you explain these patterns?

1.
6 × 9	=	54
6 × 99	=	594
6 × 999	=	5994
6 × 9999	=	59,994
6 × 99999	=	599,994
6 × 999999	=	5,999,994

2.
9 × 6	=	54
9 × 66	=	594
9 × 666	=	5994
9 × 6666	=	59,994
9 × 66666	=	599,994
9 × 666666	=	5,999,994

Compare your answers for exercises 1 and 2. Explain.

The number on the left side of the multiplication sign is multiplied by 3; the number on the right side is divided by 3, or $6 \times 9999 = (2 \times 3) \times (3 \times 3333) = (3 \times 3) \times (2 \times 3333) = 9 \times (double).$

3.
4 × 2	=	8
4 × 22	=	88
4 × 222	=	888
4 × 2222	=	8888
4 × 22222	=	88,888
4 × 222222	=	888,888

4.
2 × 4	=	8
2 × 44	=	88
2 × 444	=	888
2 × 4444	=	8888
2 × 44444	=	88,888
2 × 444444	=	888,888

Compare your answers for exercises 3 and 4. Explain.

The number on the left side of the multiplication sign is divided by 2; the number on the right side is multiplied by 2, or $4 \times 2222 = (2 \times 2) \times 2222 = 2 \times (2 \times 2222) = 2 \times 4444.$

5. Pick any two 1-digit numbers (e.g., 3 and 8).
Form a pattern similar to those in exercises 1-4.

3 × 8 =	8 × 3 =
3 × 88 =	8 × 33 =

Compare your answers and then try another example.

Detecting and explaining patterns
Understanding number properties
Developing algebraic reasoning

45

Name _____

More Pattern Power
More pattern explorations.

1. Store any 1-digit number in your calculator. Multiply by 3. Multiply by 37. Compare your answer with the original number. Explain.

e.g., 5, 15, 555

$3 \times 37 = 111$

So, $5 \times (3 \times 37) = 5 \times 111 = 555$

2. Store any 1-digit number in your calculator. Multiply by 13. Multiply by 7. Multiply by 11. Multiply by 3. Compare your answer with the starting number. Explain.

e.g., 5
65
455
3005
185,185
555,555

$13 \times 7 \times 11 \times 37 \times 3 = 111,111$

So, $5 \times (13 \times 7 \times 11 \times 37 \times 3) = 5 \times 111,111 = 555,555$

3. Store any 3-digit number in your calculator. Multiply by 13. Multiply by 7. Multiply by 11. Compare your answer with your starting number. Explain.

e.g., 123
1599
11,193
123,123

$13 \times 7 \times 11 = 1001$

So, $123 \times (13 \times 7 \times 11) = 123 \times 1001 = 123,123$

4. Store any 1-digit number in your calculator. Multiply by 16. Multiply by 43. Multiply by 1483. Look for the pattern in your answer. Explain.

e.g., 5
80
3440
5,101,520
5,101,520

$16 \times 43 \times 1483 = 1,020,304$

So, $5 \times (16 \times 43 \times 1483) = 5 \times 1,020,304 = 5,101,520$

Detecting and explaining patterns
Understanding number properties
Developing algebraic reasoning

Name _____

Super Pattern Power
Explain the patterns.

1.
$$1 \times 7 \times 11 \times 13 = 1001$$
$$2 \times 7 \times 11 \times 13 = 2002$$
$$3 \times 7 \times 11 \times 13 = 3003$$
$$4 \times 7 \times 11 \times 13 = 4004$$

Explain the pattern.

$7 \times 11 \times 13 = 1001$

$6 \times (7 \times 11 \times 13) = 6 \times 1001 = 6006$

2.
$$1 \div 11 = 0.090909$$
$$2 \div 11 = 0.181818$$
$$3 \div 11 = 0.272727$$
$$4 \div 11 = 0.363636$$
$$5 \div 11 = 0.454545$$
$$6 \div 11 = 0.545454$$

Explain the pattern.

$1 \div 11 = 0.090909; \ 6 \div 11 =$
$\quad 0.545454$

$6 \times (1 \div 11) = 6 \times 0.090909 = 0.545454$

3.
$$12,345,679 \times 9 = 111,111,111$$
$$12,345,679 \times 18 = 222,222,222$$
$$12,345,679 \times 27 = 333,333,333$$
$$12,345,679 \times 36 = 444,444,444$$
$$12,345,679 \times 45 = 555,555,555$$
$$12,345,679 \times 54 = 666,666,666$$

Explain the pattern.

$12,345,679 \times 9 = 111,111,111;$
$12,345,679 \times 63 = 12,345,679 \times (9 \times 7)$
$= (12,345,679 \times 9) \times 7 = 111,111,111 \times 7 = 777,777,777$

Detecting and explaining patterns
Understanding number properties
Developing algebraic reasoning

4.
$$2 + 4 \qquad\quad = 6 \ = 2 \times 3$$
$$2 + 4 + 6 \qquad = 12 = 3 \times 4$$
$$2 + 4 + 6 + 8 \ = 20 = 4 \times 5$$
$$2 + 4 + 6 + 8 + 10 = 30 = 5 \times 6$$

Use the graphic below to explain why $2 + 4 + 6 + 8 + 10 = 5 \times 6$.

A cut-out of the shaded part fits beside the lower piece to form a 5 x 6 rectangle.

A Little Bit Closer

Patterns

Name _____

What is a convergent sequence?

1. Use your calculator to find these decimal equivalents.

   Write the next three fractions in the sequence and their decimal equivalents.

   a. $\frac{1}{2}$ = 0.5
   b. $\frac{2}{3}$ = 0.$\overline{6}$
   c. $\frac{3}{4}$ = 0.75
   d. $\frac{4}{5}$ = 0.8
   e. $\frac{5}{6}$ = 0.8$\overline{3}$
   f. $\frac{6}{7}$ = 0.$\overline{857142}$
   g. $\frac{7}{8}$ = 0.875

   h. $\frac{8}{9}$ = 0.$\overline{8}$
   i. $\frac{9}{10}$ = 0.9
   j. $\frac{10}{11}$ = 0.$\overline{90}$

2. Mark those values above on the number line.

   0 |—————————————————————————————| 1
     $\frac{1}{2}$ $\frac{2}{3}$ $\frac{3}{4}$ $\frac{4}{5}$$\frac{5}{6}$$\frac{6}{7}$$\frac{7}{8}$$\frac{8}{9}$$\frac{9}{10}$$\frac{10}{11}$

3. What do you notice when each term is compared to the next?

   Each number is further to the right and closer to 1.

4. To what number are the sequential terms getting closer?
   How can you test that guess? _____ 1

   By testing some additional numbers, such as $\frac{86}{87}$, $\frac{233}{234}$, *etc.*

Detecting patterns
Conceptualizing limits

How Close Can You Get?

Patterns

Name _____

More about convergent sequences.

Examine this sequence: $\frac{2}{1}, \frac{3}{2}, \frac{4}{3}, \frac{5}{4}, \ldots$

1. Use your calculator to find these decimal equivalents.

   Find the next three terms in the sequence and their decimal equivalents.

   a. $\frac{2}{1}$ = 2
   b. $\frac{3}{2}$ = 1.5
   c. $\frac{4}{3}$ = 1.$\overline{3}$
   d. $\frac{5}{4}$ = 1.25
   e. $\frac{6}{5}$ = 1.2
   f. $\frac{7}{6}$ = 1.1$\overline{6}$
   g. $\frac{8}{7}$ = 1.$\overline{142857}$

   h. $\frac{9}{8}$ = 1.125
   i. $\frac{10}{9}$ = 1.$\overline{1}$
   j. $\frac{11}{10}$ = 1.1

2. Mark those values above on the number line.

   1 |—————————————————————————————| 2
   $\frac{11}{10}$$\frac{10}{9}$$\frac{9}{8}$$\frac{8}{7}$$\frac{7}{6}$$\frac{6}{5}$ $\frac{5}{4}$ $\frac{4}{3}$ 1$\frac{1}{2}$

3. What do you notice when each term in the sequence is compared to the next?

   Each number is further to the left and closer to 1.

4. To what number is the sequence getting closer? _____ 1
   This number is called the *sequence limit*.

5. Can you find a sequence that has a limit of 0? Check your guess with the calculator. What is the sequence?

   $\frac{1}{2}, \frac{1}{3}, \frac{1}{4}, \frac{1}{5}, \frac{1}{6}, \ldots$ *(other answers are possible)*

6. Can you find a sequence that has a limit of $\frac{1}{2}$? (Hint: The denominator may have to be at least twice as large as the numerator.) Check with your calculator. What is the sequence?

   $\frac{3}{5}, \frac{4}{7}, \frac{5}{9}, \frac{6}{11}, \ldots$ *(there are many other possibilities)*

Detecting patterns
Conceptualizing limits
Understanding convergent sequence

Paper Folding Challenge
Creases, pieces, lines, and numbers.

1. A point divides a line into two parts.

   Two points divide a line into how many parts?

   Complete the table on the right to show points and parts.

Number of Points	Number of Parts
1	2
2	3
3	4
4	5
6	7
82	83

2. Fold a sheet of paper in half. Fold the paper again in the same direction (see illustration). Into how many parts is the paper divided? Complete the table below.

Number of Times Folded	Number of Parts	Number of Creases
1	2	1
2	4	3
3	8	7
4	16	15
5	32	31
10	1024	1023
20	1,048,576	1,048,575

3. Fold a sheet of paper in half. Fold again in the other direction. Into how many parts is the paper divided? How many crease lines go all the way across the page? Complete the table below.

Number of Times Folded	Number of Parts	Number of Creases
1	2	1
2	4	2
3	8	3
4	16	4
5	32	5
6	64	6
20	1,048,576	20

Detecting patterns
Developing mathematical reasoning

Name

Multiplication Trick
Amaze your friends.

$$\begin{array}{r} 74 \\ \times\, 76 \\ \hline 56\ 24 \end{array}$$

$7 \times (7+1) = 7 \times 8 \rightarrow 56$

$4 \times 6 \rightarrow 24$

This trick works only if . . .
- *the one's digits add up to 10, and*
- *the ten's digits are the same.*

1. Estimate these multiplication problems in your head, using the "trick." Write the answer in the second column. Check with your calculator and write that answer in the third column.

QUESTION	ANSWER BY ESTIMATION	ANSWER BY CALCULATOR	✓
25 × 25	625		
34 × 36	1,224		
78 × 72	5616		
95 × 95	9025		
47 × 43	2021		
14 × 16	224		
61 × 69	4209		
58 × 52	3016		
45 × 45	2025		
103 × 107	11,021		

2. Create five similar exercises, completing them in your head and then with the calculator. Work with a partner to see which way is faster. Answers will vary.

Mental arithmetic
Finding patterns

Calculator Math Level E © 1995 Fearon Teacher Aids

Name _____

Remainders and the Calculator II

The easy way to find decimal remainders.

1. Find the whole number remainder.

$$6\overline{)39} \quad 6.5 \qquad 4\overline{)43} \quad 10.75 \qquad 5\overline{)62} \quad 12.4$$

R = **3**   R = **3**   R = **2**

384 ÷ 15 = 25.6. What whole number remainder does the 0.6 stand for? __**9**__

2. Find a method for determining the whole number remainder without clearing the calculator.

434 ÷ 35   **Answer:**   **12.4**

           Whole number part: **12**
           Fractional part: **.4**
           Whole number remainder: **14**

Your steps should be:

[4] [3] [4] [÷] [3] [5] [=] ([12.4 Display] [−] [1] [2]) [×] [3] [5] [=]

3. Find the quotient and remainder, using your calculator. The first one is done for you.

	Quotient	Remainder
17 ÷ 2	**8.5**	**1**
23 ÷ 4	**5.75**	**3**
184 ÷ 16	**11.5**	**8**
200 ÷ 10	**20**	**0**
163 ÷ 8	**20.375**	**3**
4403 ÷ 136	**32.375**	**51**
1239 ÷ 42	**29.5**	**21**
6734 ÷ 185	**36.4**	**74**

Developing calculator algorithms
Developing mathematical reasoning
Reviewing inverse operations

Name _____

Remainders and the Calculator I

What that decimal remainder means.

1. Complete these division problems in longhand. Leave a remainder. The first one is done for you.

a. $4\overline{)30}$ **7 R2**
    28
    —
    2

b. $5\overline{)23}$ **4 R3**
    20
    —
    3

c. $8\overline{)46}$ **5 R6**
    40
    —
    6

d. $4\overline{)38}$ **9 R2**
    36
    —
    2

2. Complete these division problems in longhand. Use decimals. Check with your calculator. The first one is done for you.

a. $4\overline{)30.0}$ **7.5**
    28
    —
    20
    20
    —
    0

b. $5\overline{)23.0}$ **4.6**
    20
    —
    30
    30
    —
    0

c. $8\overline{)46.00}$ **5.75**
    40
    —
    60
    56
    —
    40
    40
    —
    0

d. $4\overline{)38.0}$ **9.5**
    36
    —
    20
    20
    —
    0

Compare problems **1a** and **2a**.
Use the decimal quotient to find the remainder.

$$\begin{array}{r} 7.5 \\ \times\ 4 \\ \hline 30.0 \end{array}$$

or

$7.5 \times 4 = (7 + 0.5) \times 4 = (7 \times 4) + (0.5 \times 4)$
                    $= 28 + ②$ Remainder
                    $= 30$

Use your calculator to find the remainder from the decimal quotient.
Write down which buttons you push to check the remainders for problems **b**, **c**, and **d** above.

(b). **.6 x 5 =**

(c). **.75 x 8 =**

(d). **.5 x 4 =**

Developing calculator algorithms
Developing mathematical reasoning
Reviewing inverse operations

Name _____

Remainders and the Calculator III

Test your skill with remainders.

1. Multiply. Work out longhand.

$$\frac{1}{8} \times 8 \qquad \frac{4}{9} \times 9 \qquad \frac{2}{3} \times 3$$

$$= 1 \qquad = 4 \qquad = 2$$

2. Change to decimals.

$$\frac{1}{8} = 0.3 \qquad \frac{4}{9} = 0.4 \qquad \frac{2}{3} = 0.6$$

3. Repeat these problems, using your calculator.

$$\frac{1}{8} \times 3 \qquad \frac{4}{9} \times 9 \qquad \frac{2}{3} \times 6$$

$$= 0.9999996 \qquad = 3.9999996 \qquad = 3.9999996$$

4. Compare the answers from the problems in exercises 1 and 3.
Which answers are correct?

The answers to question 1.

| When the calculator displays 0.9999999, it usually means 1. |

5. Find the quotient and whole number remainder for these division problems.

	Quotient	Remainder
62 ÷ 3	20	2
73 ÷ 9	8	1
84 ÷ 13	6	6
127 ÷ 7	18	1
135 ÷ 19	7	2
236 ÷ 21	11	5
6087 ÷ 89	68	35
2111 ÷ 17	124	3

Developing calculator algorithms
Developing mathematical reasoning
Reviewing inverse operations

For activity sheet "Going in Circles I" on page 55, answers will vary.

Calculator Math Level E © 1995 Fearon Teacher Aids

Chess Master

Just a few grains of rice.

Name _____

This is a famous tale about the game of chess.
The game's inventor presented it to his king and queen who were totally thrilled by the game. As a reward, they offered him anything he wanted, expecting he would ask for a bag of diamonds or bars of gold. Instead, the seemingly insignificant reward the inventor asked for was:

"1 grain of rice for the first square on the chess board, 2 for the second, 4 for the third, 8 for the fourth, and so on."

The king and queen granted his request immediately. They thought all the man wanted was a few bags of rice. Boy, were they wrong!

Complete the table, showing the rice required for the FIRST TWO ROWS on the chess board.

SQUARE	CALCULATION	GRAINS OF RICE
1	1	1
2	1 x 2	2
3	2 x 2	4
4	2 x 2 x 2	8
5	2 x 2 x 2 x 2	16
6	2 x 2 x 2 x 2 x 2	32
7	2 x 2 x 2 x 2 x 2 x 2	64
8	etc.	128
9		256
10		512
11		1024
12		2048
13		4096
14		8192
15		16,384
16		32,768

Exponents

56

Best Buys

Who's the smartest shopper?

Name _____

Circle the "best buys" for each item.

ITEM	BRAND A		BRAND B	
	Size	Cost	Size	Cost
Chips	50 g	20¢	40 g	19¢
Onions	1 kg	39¢	1.5 kg	50¢
Pickles	750 mL	2 for $1.49	800 mL	3 for $2.09
Hamburger	800 g	$1.47	900 g	$1.60
Cheese	0.5 kg pack	2 packs for $1.49	0.75 kg pack	$1.07
Apples	10	98¢ a dozen	10	2 for 19¢
Jelly	50 mL	3 for 89¢	25 mL	7 for $1.00
Pop	300 mL	6 for $1.49	750 mL	33¢ each
Bread	500 g	3 for $1.45	750 g	2 for $1.45
Soap	100 g	2 for 63¢	150 g	3 for 99¢

Working with ratio
Developing consumer awareness
Using the calculator judiciously

57

89

For activity sheet "One of Everything" on page 58, answers will vary.

Name _____

Batter Up!

Who's the best batter?

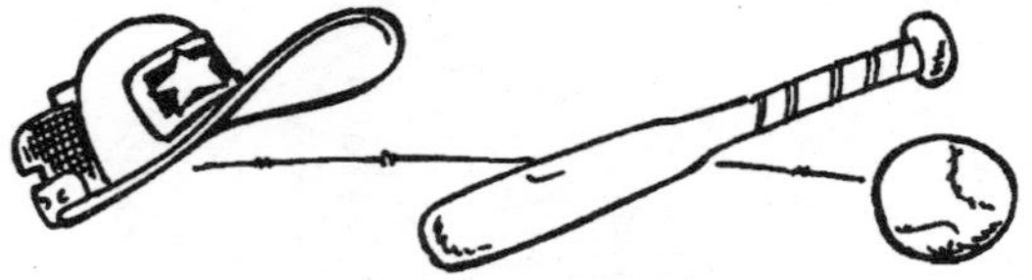

Complete the table.
(Calculations for the first line are shown below.)

Name	Hits	Times at Bat	Batting Average
Jones	84	304	0.276
Berstein	95	310	0.306
Duncan	83	340	0.244
Washington	96	295	0.325
Kew	26	141	0.184
Park	37	162	0.228
Brown	121	351	0.345
Kolinski	134	400	0.335
Suavé	85	304	0.280
Totals	**761**	**2607**	**0.292**

Team Average

Jones' Batting Average = Hits ÷ Times at Bat
= 84 ÷ 304
= 0.2763157
= 0.276

1. Which player would be the best choice for your team? Explain.

Brown: highest average (see Teacher's Guide)

2. Can the team average be found in two ways? Explain.

See Teacher's Guide

Finding and evaluating averages
Discerning the basis for an average

59

Faster Than a Speeding Snail (Graph)

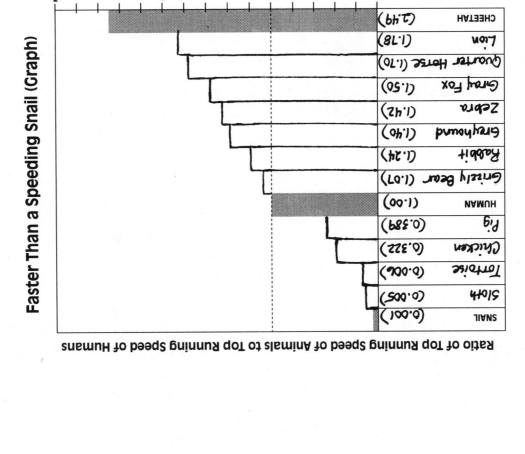

Ratio of Top Running Speed of Animals to Top Running Speed of Humans

CHEETAH	(2.49)
Lion	(1.78)
Quarter Horse	(1.70)
Gray Fox	(1.50)
Zebra	(1.42)
Greyhound	(1.40)
Rabbit	(1.24)
Grizzly Bear	(1.07)
HUMAN	(1.00)
Pig	(0.389)
Chicken	(0.322)
Tortoise	(0.006)
Sloth	(0.005)
SNAIL	(0.001)

For activity sheet "If the Shoe Fits" on page 60, answers will vary depending on the number of family members and data collected.

Name _____

Thinking Through the Problem

Plan your strategy.

1. How could you get the number "5" in your calculator display using only the ⊞ ⊟ ⊠ ⊞ and ② keys?

   $2 + 2 + 2 - 2 + 2 \div 2$

2. Light travels at a speed of 297,650 km/second. How far is that in one hour?

   $1,071,540,000 \ km$

3. If today was your 12th birthday, how many days old would you be?

   $4383 \ days$

4. How would you find 432 × 725 on your calculator if neither the ③ nor the ④ keys were working?

   $2 \times 216 \times 725$

5. During figure skating competition, Peggy obtained these scores: 9.5, 8.7, 8.4, and 8.8. What was her average score?

   8.85

6. A complicated computer job is estimated to take a million seconds. How long is that (in minutes/hours/days/weeks)? $1 \ day, \ 3 \ hours, \ 46.8 \ minutes$

7. The price tag for a soda pop sale reads "3/$1.00." How much would it cost you to buy five cans? $\$1.67$

8. How old will you be (in years) when you are 5000 days old?

   $13.7 \ years \ or \ 13 \ years, \ 8 \ months$

9. The annual membership fee at a golf club went up from $400 to $500. The cost per game went down from $12 to $8. After how many games are the new rates better?

   $After \ 25 \ games$

Analyzing problems

For activity sheet "Soda Pop Challenge" on page 63, answers will vary depending on the data collected.

Calculator Math Level E © 1995 Fearon Teacher Aids

Name _____

Money Matters

How good are you with money?

1. Up in Smoke

Find out the cost of a pack of cigarettes. What would it cost to buy one pack daily for:

1 year? _**Answers will vary**_   40 years? _____

Check with a person who smokes to find out how many packs per day he or she smokes. Compute his or her smoking cost per year.

2. Heavy Expenses

Find the mass of each item.

penny: _3.25_ g
nickel: _4.5_ g
dime: _.2_ g
quarter: _5_ g
dollar bill: _1_ g

Calculate the mass of $100 in:

pennies: _32.5 kg_
nickels: _9 kg_
dimes: _2 kg_
quarters: _2 kg_
dollar bills: _0.1 kg_

3. Discount Baby-sitting

Bill's Baby Business is announcing a special for November. Baby-sitting rates are $1.00 per hour for the first child, half of that for the second child, half of the cost of the second child for the third child, and so on.

a. Find Bill's rate per hour for 2 children. _$1.50_

b. For 3 children. _$1.75_

c. For 6 children. _$1.97_

d. What is his maximum rate per hour? _$2.00_

Collecting data
Finding the mass of an object
Conceptualizing limits
Finding rates

66

For activity sheet "A Day in Your Life" on page 65, answers will vary depending on the data collected.

Name _____

Going in Circles II

Solve problems working with pi.

1. The world record for Ferris wheel riding is 21 days, 3 hours, and 58 minutes. During that time, the rider traveled 1158.728 km (in circles) in 11,800 revolutions.

   a. What was the diameter of the wheel? **31.96 m**

   b. How long did the wheel take to travel one revolution? **2.58 min, or 2 min, 35s**

   c. How long did the rider take to travel one km? **26.25 min or 26 min, 15s**

   d. What was the speed of the wheel in revolutions per minute? **0.39 rev. per min.**

   e. What was the speed of the rider in kilometers per hour? **2.28 km/h**

2. You need a new tire for your car. The tire you decide to buy is steel-belted and treadwear-rated at 40,000 km.

     Cost: $67.50   **Diameter:** 83 cm

     Cost per kilometer = **0.0016875**

     Number of revolutions required to go 40,000 km = **15,340,234**

Working with pi
Working with ratios
Finding rates of speed

Name _____

Burger Business

Work with larger facts.

A certain hamburger chain claims to have sold 20,000,000,000 hamburgers. The average hamburger has 100 g of meat, 2.5 mL of ketchup, and 0.3 g of salt.

1. If a cow yields 150 kg of beef, how many cows were needed for these hamburgers? **13,333,333**

2. How many tanker trucks, each holding 6 m³, would be needed to deliver the ketchup? **8.334 (last truck only 1/3 full)**

3. How many tons of salt were used? **6,000 tons**

For Experts

Create your own problem about the pickles or onions found in some of the hamburgers. Give this problem to a classmate to solve.

Working with large numbers
Working with ratios

Calculator Math Level E © 1995 Fearon Teacher Aids

Calculator Math Level E © 1995 Fearon Teacher Aids

Name _____

Hummingbird Trivia

Discover some incredible numbers.

Some Facts About Hummingbirds

▶ The giant hummingbird grows up to 21 cm long and weighs 20 g. The bee hummingbird is 6.25 cm long and weighs 2 g.

▶ A hummingbird's tongue licks nectar at a rate of 13 licks per second. It can lick 3-8 g of nectar from a feeder at one time.

▶ Hummingbirds eat more than half their body weight in food and drink eight times their weight in water each day.

▶ Hummingbirds need 6660 to 12,400 calories per day. They use 35 calories per minute to hover. (Humans need about 2500 kilo calories per day, i.e., 2,500,000 "hummingbird" calories.)

▶ Hummingbird hearts beat from 480 to 1260 times per minute. They breathe about 250 times per minute. (Humans breathe about 16 times per minute.)

▶ Ruby-throated hummingbirds fly at up to 48 km per hour (they can dive at 128 km/h). Their wings beat an average of 52 times per second.

▶ Ruby-throated hummingbirds migrate up to 3200 km (Nova Scotia to Panama), including an 800 km non-stop trip over open ocean. A ruby-throat can fly for up to 26 hours before landing.

▶ Hummingbird eggs are less than 1.25 cm long and weigh less than 5 g.

Problems

1. How many times will a ruby-throated hummingbird's heart beat in an hour?

2. How many heartbeats will the ruby-throated hummingbird experience during its non-stop ocean crossing? How many breaths? How many wing beats?

3. A full grown ostrich weighs about 140 kg. How many bee hummingbirds would it take to weigh the same?

Using these hummingbird facts, create some problems of your own to exchange with a classmate. See if you can solve them.

1. From 28,800 to 75,600 beats per hour.
2. 748,800 to 1,965,600 heartbeats, 390,000 breaths, 189,153,120 wing beats.
3. 70,000

Integration with science
Reading carefully for information
Problem solving

69

Name _____

For Calculating Experts

Now that you're an expert. . . .

1. Find 888 × 88 on your calculator without using the 8 key. $4 \times 4444 \times 44$

2. Use your calculator to find the remainders for these division problems.

 a. 89 ÷ 8 $((89 \div 8) - 11) \times 8 = 1$

 b. 75 ÷ 6 $((75 \div 6) - 12) \times 6 = 3$

 c. 29 ÷ 3 $((29 \div 3) - 9) \times 3 = 2$

 d. 539 ÷ 29 $((539 \div 29) - 18) \times 29 = 17$

 e. 7931 ÷ 267 $(7931 \div 267) - 29 \times 267 = 188$

3. Use each of the digits [1] [2] [3] [4] [5] [6] [7] [8] once to make two 4-digit numbers with the largest possible product. $8531 \times 7642 = 65,193,902$

4. Use each of the digits [1] [2] [3] [4] [5] [6] [7] [8] once to make two 4-digit numbers with the smallest possible product. $1357 \times 2468 = 3,349,076$

5. Use each of the digits [2] [3] [4] [5] [6] [7] once to make two numbers with the largest possible product. (You can make this problem easier by changing it to one with an even number of digits.) $73 \times 642 = 46,866$

6. Use each of the digits [2] [3] [4] [5] [6] [7] once to make two numbers with the smallest possible product. $36 \times 247 = 8892$

7. Use each of the digits [1] [2] [3] [4] [5] [6] [7] [8] [9] once to make three 3-digit numbers with the largest possible product. $941 \times 852 \times 763 = 611,721,516$

8. Use each of the digits [1] [2] [3] [4] [5] [6] [7] [8] [9] once to make three 3-digit numbers with the smallest possible product. $147 \times 258 \times 369 = 13,994,694$

95

Name _____

Friends in Numbers
Working with number patterns.

1. Three people give each other birthday presents. How many presents are there all together?
What if there had been four people? Fill in the chart.

Number of People	Number of Presents
2	2
3	6
4	12
5	20
6	30
8	56
10	90
18	306

Can you find a formula that gives the number of presents for any group of people?

2. Three people are introduced to each other and shake hands.
How many handshakes are there all together? What if there had been four people?
Complete the chart to show the number of handshakes for other groups.

Number of People	Number of Shakes
2	1
3	3
4	6
5	10
6	15
8	28
10	45
18	153

Can you find a formula that gives the number of handshakes for any group of people?

Developing algebraic reasoning